WAYMARK

RED · GUIDE

HAMPSHIRE

BARRY SHURLOCK

Romsey in the mud,
Southampton on the stones,
Winchester eats the meat,
Andover picks the bones.

TRADITIONAL

RED GUIDE
HAMPSHIRE

BARRY SHURLOCK

FOR MALCOLM AND TOM

AUTHOR
Barry Shurlock

ILLUSTRATOR
Mark Peppé

COVER ILLUSTRATION
Glyn Dawson

EDITING
First Edition

TOWN INFORMATION PANELS
Vijay Patel; additional work by Virginia Langer

CARTOGRAPHY
© *The Automobile Association 1989*

Typeset by
Avonset, Midsomer Norton, Bath

Printed and bound by
Richard Clay Limited, Bungay,
Suffolk

The contents of this publication
are believed correct at the time of
printing. Nevertheless, the
Publishers cannot accept
responsibility for errors or
omissions, nor for changes in
details given.

Published by
Waymark Publications,
an imprint of The
Automobile Association

© The Automobile Association 1989

Produced and distributed in the
United Kingdom by the
Publishing Division of
The Automobile Association,
Fanum House, Basingstoke,
Hampshire RG21 2EA

ISBN 0 86145 8087

HOW TO USE THIS BOOK

The *Red Guide Hampshire* divides the county into six sections. These sections are divided again into smaller areas to explore. Most of the smaller areas begin with a description of the largest town, or another good place to start a tour. This is followed by an exploration of the surrounding area.

The map on pages 6–7 shows starting points for local tours, with page numbers.

A complete, alphabetical list of all the places in the book is given in the index at the end of the book, together with suggestions for further reading.

Town information panels

Practical information is given for selected towns. This includes early closing and market days, cashpoints, tourist information centres, places to visit, leisure centres, cinemas, and access by road and rail. Places to visit which are closed for much of the year, or which only open on a few days of the week are marked *. At the time of going to press, places not marked with an asterisk were open all year round, and on most days of the week. Tourist information centres will have details of any changes.

For information on places mentioned elsewhere in the book, contact local tourist information offices, or the regional tourist board: Southern Tourist Board, 40 Chamberlayne Road, Eastleigh, Hampshire SO5 5JH.

Or see The Automobile Association's annual guide to places to visit in Britain.

Other useful addresses:
English Heritage, 23 Savile Row, London W1X 2BT

Hampshire and Isle of Wight Naturalists' Trust, 71 The Hundred, Romsey, Hampshire SO51 8BZ

National Trust,
36 Queen Anne's Gate,
London SW1H 9AS

National Gardens Scheme
(private gardens opened occasionally to the public),
57 Lower Belgrave Street,
London SW1W 0LR.
Annual booklet available in shops in spring.

Royal Society for Protection of Birds (RSPB), The Lodge, Sandy, Beds SG19 2DL

Royal Society for Nature Conservation (RSNC), The Green, Nettleham, Lincoln LN2 2NR

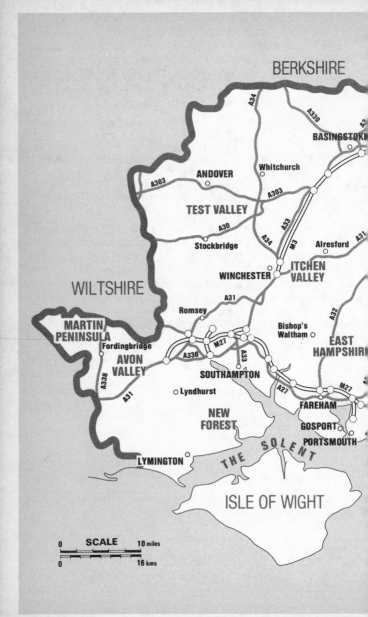

CONTENTS

INTRODUCTION

HAMPSHIRE CAN LAY claim to being the heart of southern England. Facing the Isle of Wight, which was once part of it, it is contained on the mainland by Dorset, Wiltshire, Berkshire, Surrey and Sussex. It is beyond question a vital link between London and the Channel – Southampton and Portsmouth have long had close connections with the metropolis; while Winchester, the seat of the County Council, listens more to the pulse of the countryside.

Most of Hampshire sits on thin chalk soils, on high downs cut by clear streams. But much of its character comes from the more intractable soils that lie off the chalk, particularly those of the Hampshire Basin to the south. The agricultural poverty of the New Forest (and the Dorset heaths) is one of the reasons why this vast tract of land has survived in a wild state. Poor soils also account for the barrenness of the Solent shores and the relatively late development of South Hampshire. Similarly, the extension of the western edge of the Weald to East Hampshire explains the special character of the hanger

country, where the beds of the upper greensand have been eroded to give dramatic wooded slopes.

This is a rich county with a treasure-house of memories and associations – the county of Jane Austen and Flora Thompson, of the Duke of Wellington and Earl Mountbatten.

Winchester, which is included in the first section of the book, still trades on the fact that it was the Saxon capital of England. The surrounding countryside is typical of the valleys of the Hampshire chalk streams: the upper reaches of the River Itchen and the valley of the Candover Stream are a delight.

The second and third sections of the guide cover the cities of Portsmouth and Southampton and their hinterlands. They are very different cities, one dominated by the Royal Navy, the other reflecting influences of commercial shipping and yachting. Similarly, the shingle beaches of the east Solent are a world away from the muddy shores of the west side of Southampton Water.

Portsmouth's influence spreads to Havant and the

seaside resort of Hayling Island, and extends along the A3 corridor into east Hampshire. But this part of Hampshire is kept separate from the coast by the chalk ridges of the South Downs; they hide a countryside which is remarkably intimate and unspoilt.

The main town of East Hampshire, Petersfield, is the gateway to the hanger country. Dramatic hills and a rich mosaic of small villages and woodlands makes this area one of the treasures of Hampshire – and it is relatively unknown.

The fourth section covers the New Forest, an area of open heaths and woodland which, although managed by man, is the wildest place in the south of England, and extends up the valley of the Avon to Fordingbridge and beyond.

The Test valley is a fabulous place whose main towns are Andover and Romsey; but its character comes from its villages – places like Houghton, Leckford, Wherwell and Longparish. Underpinned by wealthy newcomers, this well-manicured part of Hampshire seems like one great garden.

The influence of London suburban pressures are greatest in the fast-growing Basingstoke area. Since the 1960s Basingstoke town has been virtually rebuilt and it now commands a part of Hampshire where a strong presence of industry and the military is apparent: Aldershot Military Town is sandwiched between the civilian town to the south and the 'airman's Mecca' of Farnborough to the north. Threading through the countryside is the Basingstoke Canal, a commercial misfortune that has become a major leisure asset, passing through some extremely pretty countryside. The North Hampshire Downs to the north-west of Basingstoke are indisputably part of the county, but their dramatic heights, which include Watership Down, look out upon a landscape that drains to the Thames: a different world.

ACKNOWLEDGEMENTS

Writing a guide such as this involves help from a large variety of sources. I am most grateful to all the Tourist Information Officers and museum staff who, knowingly or otherwise, assisted in the gathering of material for the book. The knowledge and good conversation of the many people who accompanied me in the task of covering the county is gratefully acknowledged.

BCS

1 Winchester and the Itchen Valley

Winchester is an ideal centre. Not only is it geographically in the middle of Hampshire; it also has extremely good communications with every part of the county. Within Winchester are the offices of all the most important administrative functions of county government and the law.

Winchester is a very traditional city: the 20th century is celebrated elsewhere. Even when the poet John Keats stayed here in the early years of the last century he felt obliged to describe the streets as 'excessively maidenlike'. Some of them still are, particularly in the south east of the city, in the vicinity of the cathedral and Winchester College.

Wintonians take a long-term view of things and relish the quiet security of the English way of life. Visitors in search of a dependable heritage flock to the city (actually the size of a modest town), as they flock to Oxford, Salisbury, York and Edinburgh. The cathedral, Winchester's original *raison d'être*, still is its greatest attraction. The faithful, and those interested in history, flood its aisles. Even the 'lager louts' favour its green.

The story of Winchester follows a familiar pattern. During the Iron Age there was a hill-fort at the top of St Catherine's Hill and another settlement in the Oram's Arbour area of the city. Then the Romans built a military town in the valley. At the end of the Roman era the town declined dramatically and Saxon mercenaries started to settle in the area. In the middle of the 7th century a Christian church was built and became the *cathedra* of the West Saxon bishop.

Winchester came to prominence as a royal centre in the late 9th century, when the large Saxon town at *Southampton* came under serious threat from Viking attacks. The relationship between Southampton as a port and Winchester as a seat of power continues, to some degree, to the present day. Winchester is nourished by the whole of Hampshire, but particularly by the south coast, which can be seen (together with the chimneys of Fawley's refinery) from several viewpoints around the city.

Southampton is 'town' and Winchester is indisputably 'country'. And what country! The chalk streams and meadows of central Hampshire are a delight, particularly in the summer. The clear waters that ooze in an endless stream from the chalk are rich in nutrients. The rivers support an abundant flora and fauna and are famed for their trout. Watching a skilled fisherman control a long length of line in the air, and then lightly drop the fly beside his quarry, is itself one of the joys of the Winchester countryside.

The villages around Winchester are almost a cliché: thatched cottages, with roses round the door, are commonplace. Most of them have long been in the hands of commuters, but the villages along the Candover Valley, and in the upper Itchen Valley, are still remarkably unspoilt.

If Winchester and its country has a fault, it is perhaps that of being too peaceful, even a little complacent. Peace, contemplation and order are high priorities in this part of Hampshire. Perhaps the ghost of Isaac Walton still walks. He lived with his son-in-law in the close of Winchester Cathedral and, one suspects, enjoyed nothing more than good conversation beside the babbling waters of the Itchen, an arm of which skirts the deanery garden. Raw excitement is hard to find in this particular part of Hampshire. If thrills are a priority, it might be best to look elsewhere. Winchester is the uncompromising heart of rural Hampshire.

Winchester Cathedral

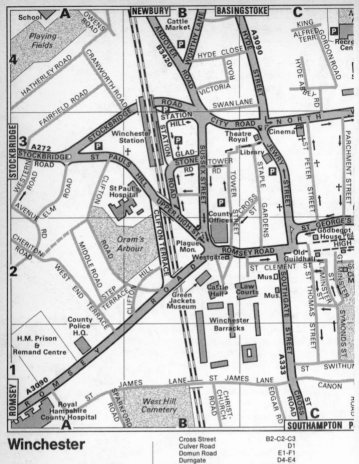

Winchester

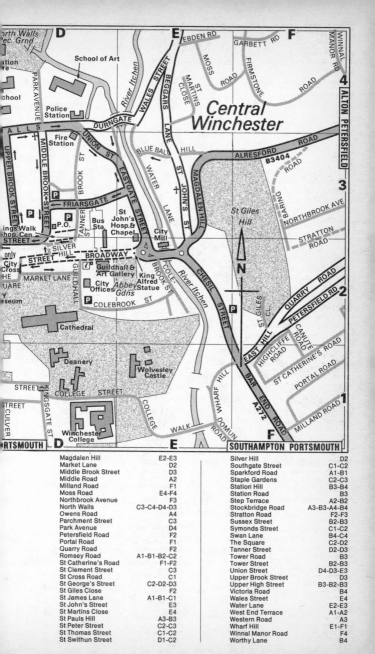

Central Winchester

Hampshire local government

As in all other parts of the country, the County Council for Hampshire was created by statute in 1888. Its first meeting was held in the Great Hall, Winchester, on 7 February 1889, when its elected members were called to order under the interim chairmanship of the sheriff, William Wickham. The council then elected 25 aldermen, many from the 'old families' of the county.

The first chairman of the council was the Liberal Lord Basing, who lived near Odiham and as George Sclater-Booth, MP for North Hampshire, had played an important part in creating local government as it is today.

Before the creation of the county council, local affairs were governed by Justices at the Quarter Sessions and by a plethora of special boards.

One of the first tasks of the new county council was to set up the hierarchy of district and parish councils that survived with only minor changes until the local government reorganisation of 1974. A major feature of the old system was that Portsmouth and Southampton were then county boroughs, and as such were self-governing.

The creation of parish councils in 1894 was a development which in many places appeared to threaten the local squirearchy. Some parish councils could not be formed, because there were either no candidates, or no voters!

WINCHESTER

This famous cathedral city has been the main administrative centre of Hampshire for at least 1,200 years. Its proud boast is that it was also once the capital of England. This came about because Winchester was a very important place in Wessex, the West Saxon kingdom whose leaders, in the centuries before the Norman Conquest, united the English kingdom. A visit to Winchester is therefore an exercise in English history. But it is one in which viewing the sights can be laced with a meal at a pleasant restaurant or a visit to fine shops – in the Square, the High Street, Broadway and Parchment Street, Jewry Street and elsewhere. A quick introduction to the city can be found at the Winchester Heritage Centre in Upper Brook Street.

A casual look at the plan of the city will show that it is made up of a grid of streets, as regular as that of Manhattan. The spine of the grid is High Street, which is best seen from the east: it is dominated by the great bracket clock outside the Old Guildhall (now Lloyds Bank) and the West Gate at the top of the hill. This was once one of the main entrances through the walls that encircled the city. Since 1067 the high ground hereabouts has held the secular seat of power. Here are the headquarters of the Hampshire County Council, and the law courts, where many trials of national significance have been, and still are, held. Until recently this was also the home of the Royal Green Jackets, the Light Division, which still has a museum on the site (the barracks are now a mile to the north of the city, at Flowerdown).

The original seat of power in the town lay in the south-east corner, where the Romans had their forum and the Saxon bishop and king had their palaces. The Diocese of Winchester originally stretched from the south bank of the Thames to the Solent. At its heart was the famous cathedral, which has been an object of pilgrimage for well over 1,000 years. It is still the best place to start a tour of Winchester.

The most impressive view of the cathedral is from the west. The great west front dates from the end of the 14th century: the intricate tracery of its windows and gable represents the height of the power of the medieval bishopric, in the person of William of Wickham (bishop 1366–1404).

It helps to appreciate the inside of the cathedral if you first walk round the outside. A pleasant footpath starts at the south-west corner and runs all the way round, past the south wall of the nave (with its early 20th-century buttressing), through a tunnel under the south transept (11th century) to the east end of the cathedral (13th century), then into Colebrook Street and past the modern Wessex Hotel. From here there is a superb view of the Norman stonework of the north transept (11th century) and the two lines of windows which Wickham inserted on both sides of the nave in the late 14th century. The two most westerly windows are rather dumpy, reflecting the style of his predecessor, William Edington (bishop 1345–65), who had started to remodel the cathedral.

On the turf alongside the north wall of the cathedral are marked the lines of the Saxon minster that was replaced by the present building towards the end of the 11th century. The first church at Winchester was founded in the middle of the 7th century, shortly before the seat of the West Saxon see, created in 635, came here from Dorchester-on-Thames. The details of the elaborate minster that the Normans demolished to make way for their own church are explained on a permanent display beside the turf, and in the City Museum, which is on the north side of the cathedral green. The museum also contains many other displays on the history of the

Winchester

Population: 35,644

Early Closing: Thu

Market Days: Wed, Fri, Sat

Cashpoints: *Barclays* 50 Jewry St; *Lloyds* 49 High St; *Midland* 58 High St; *NatWest* 105 High St, Andover Rd

Tourist Information: The Guildhall, Broadway

Attractions: City Museum, Great Hall of Winchester Castle, Hospital of St Cross, Royal Hussars Museum*, Serle's House, Westgate Museum, Winchester College, Pilgrims Hall

Arts: Art School Gallery, Attic Theatre, Guildhall Gallery, Theatre Royal, Tower Arts Centre

Leisure: River Park Leisure Centre

By Road: London 64 miles (M3), Southampton 13 miles (A33)

By Rail: 1hr 5mins from London (Waterloo to Weymouth line). Direct services to Basingstoke, Eastleigh and Southampton

1 West Front
2 Nave
3 North Aisle
4 South Aisle
5 Choir
6 North Transept
7 Presbytery
8 High Altar
9 Retrochoir
10 Guardian Angels' Chapel
11 Lady Chapel
12 Langton Chapel
13 South Transept
14 Epiphany Chapel

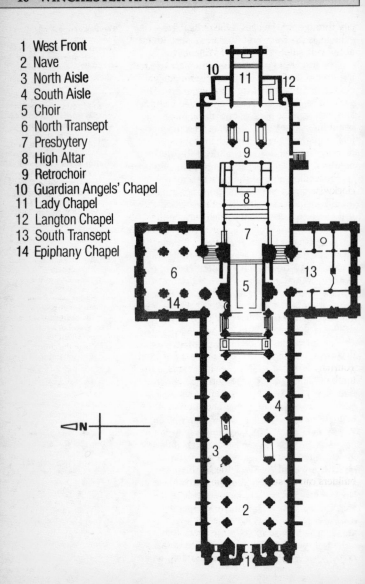

city throughout the ages. One of its prize exhibits is the Sparsholt Roman mosaic, found at the villa site to the west of Winchester.

The inside of the cathedral is remarkable for its sheer size. There is still no other medieval church in Europe that can rival its length. The great nave, with its elaborately carved columns and lofty vaulted roof, is one of the most beautiful in the world. It also represents a great feat of engineering, for Wickham's masons literally 'applied it' to the fabric of the Norman building.

Proceeding around the cathedral in a clockwise direction, the first points of interest are the memorials to the Rifle Brigade and the King's Royal Rifle Corps (which became the Royal Green Jackets) at the west end. Also at the west end is the cathedral treasury, which has displays of church plate and artefacts from excavations of the Saxon minster. Jane Austen's grave lies on the floor of the north aisle. This remarkable lady, who came to Winchester in her last months, is also commemorated by a memorial on the wall nearby and by a stained-glass window.

Further east is the cathedral's great decorated font, which is carved in marble from Tournai, Belgium. Beside the choir steps is the tomb of George Morley (bishop 1662–84), the first bishop to serve after the episcopal hiatus that followed the Civil War. The choir itself contains the tomb of William Rufus, William II, who was killed during a hunting trip in the *New Forest*. The choir stalls date from 1308 and are the oldest series in England.

The powerful arches of the Norman builders can be seen to their best advantage in the north transept. On the south side of the transept is the Holy Sepulchre Chapel, where medieval wall paintings of international significance can be seen. In the south-east corner of the transept is the entrance to the crypt, open only in the summer months, when

The Saxon minster, Winchester

The first Christian church in Winchester was built in the mid-7th century. It was as long as the present cathedral is wide. Called the Old Minster or the Saxon Minster, it remained virtually unchanged until the 10th century, when it was extended under the hand of Aethelwold (bishop 963–86), whose statue is on the altar screen of the present cathedral. He was born in Winchester and came back after serving at the abbeys of Glastonbury and Abingdon, where he was abbot. One of his first acts was to replace the canons of the Old Minster, who had fallen into worldly ways, with monks from his former monastery.

Aethelwold wanted to honour St Swithun by bringing his grave, which had (at his own request) originally been sited outside the west end of the minster, within the structure of the church. He therefore built out the west end, and shortly afterwards extended the east end and provided it with a crypt.

During Aethelwold's episcopate the Old Minster shared in the great cultural awakening that was spreading throughout Europe. Religious manuscripts were embellished in a style that is called the Winchester School.

The site of the Old Minster overlaps the present cathedral, the line of which dips strongly to the south.

the water table is lowest! It contains a 'holy well'. Here were kept the remains of the Saxon kings of Wessex and of England, until in the 12th century they were gathered up and placed in chests on the top of the presbytery screens, to the east of the choir. They are still there, albeit slightly mixed up. On the north side are said to be the remains of Kenulph, Egbert and Edmund (son of Alfred the Great), whilst on the south are those of Kynegils, Ethelwulf, Edred, Canute and others.

Close to the high altar is the chantry of Stephen Gardiner (bishop 1531–55), one of the several chantries for which Winchester is noted. These were small chapels built around the graves of bishops, where monks said prayers for the prelate. In the Anglo-Catholic tradition of Winchester, Gardiner opposed the changes of the Reformation. In 1553 he was restored to the bishopric by Mary Tudor, whom he married to Philip of Spain in the cathedral in the following year.

To the east of Gardiner's chantry is the more elaborate chantry of William Waynflete (bishop 1446–86), headmaster of Winchester College and the first provost of Eton College, which was modelled on it. He was also the founder of Magdalene College, Oxford. To the south of Waynflete's chantry is that of Henry Beaufort (bishop 1404–47). He was the illegitimate son of John of Gaunt and sat on the tribunal that condemned Joan of Arc to be burnt. A statue of the French heroine stands to the east of the bishop's chantry. It was erected in 1923, the year in which she was canonised.

The east end of the original Norman cathedral built by Walkelin (bishop 1069–1107) ended at a point between the chantries of Gardiner and Waynflete. It was here that the sacred relics of St Swithun were kept. It was the growing popularity of this saintly man that provided one of the main reasons for later extensions of the east end – to provide room

Isaak Walton window, Winchester Cathedral

STUDY TO BE QUIET

for the crush of pilgrims. At the end of the 12th century Godfrey of Lucy (bishop 1189–1204) built the lovely retrochoir and lady chapel, which are some of the finest examples of Early English architecture. The site of the shrine of St Swithun is marked by a 20th-century canopy. Like all bishops of Winchester before the Dissolution, Swithun (bishop 837–62) was also head of the cathedral priory, which subsequently took his name.

The tiny Guardian Angels' Chapel in the north-east corner of the cathedral contains the tomb of Peter Mews (bishop 1684–1706), who fought in the battle of Sedgemoor. To the south is the much larger Lady Chapel, which contains the chair that Mary Tudor used at her marriage in the cathedral. The chapel is much used by the Mothers' Union, which was founded at *Alresford*, near Winchester, by Mary Sumner. The novelist Charlotte Yonge (1823–1901), who also lived near Winchester, is commemorated by gifts of furnishings. The Langton Chapel to the south is named after Stephen Langton (bishop 1492–1502). At its entrance stands a statue of the diver William Walker, who underpinned the east end of the cathedral in the early years of the present century. To the west of Beaufort's chantry is probably the most beautiful chantry in the whole cathedral, that of Richard Fox (bishop 1502–29), founder of Corpus Christi College, Oxford. Pilgrims visiting St Swithun's shrine at the east end of the cathedral were kept from the nave, the monks' church, by the medieval iron gates which still hang at the entrance to the south transept.

The transept includes the Silkstede Chapel, where Isaac Walton (1593–1683), author of the *Compleat Angler*, was buried. There is a stained-glass window erected in his memory by fishermen. It includes the famous motto: 'Study to be quiet'. At the centre of the transept is a statue of Samuel Wilberforce (bishop

Saint Swithun
Although originally dedicated to St Peter and St Paul, it is the dedication of Winchester Cathedral to St Swithun (bishop 837–62) that gives it its ecclesiastical personality. The saintly reputation of this man, who was born at Winchester, followed him after his death, so much so that lying on his grave was said to effect miraculous cures.

On St Swithun's Day, 15 July, prospects for the summer can be forecast:

St Swithun's Day, if thou be fair,
For forty days it will remain.
St Swithun's Day, if thou bring rain,
For forty days it will remain.

The tradition of St Swithun's Day is based on the fact that a long period of rain followed the translation of the saint's remains into the Saxon Minster on 15 July 971.

St Swithun's shrine became a popular subject of pilgrimage during the 10th century. The Normans were keen to retain its popularity and it was therefore transferred to the present cathedral at its dedication in 1093. The annals say that 'on the very next day' workmen started to pull down the Old Minster.

St Swithun's shrine was taken down after the dissolution of the cathedral priory in 1539. The canopy which now marks the position of the shrine is a modern creation. The broken egg-shell motifs which it includes recall the legend that Swithun once restored eggs dropped by a fellow Wintonian.

William of Wickham

This great bishop of Winchester (bishop 1366–1404) was humbly born at Wickham, near Fareham. William Long, as he was baptised, was recognised as a clever lad and sent to the priory school at Winchester. At the age of 14 he became secretary to his mentor, lord of the manor of Wickham, who was also the Constable of Winchester Castle. William was later introduced to Edward III by the bishop of the day, William of Edington, and thereafter pursued a brilliant career in the king's service. He first served as a surveyor and architect and was involved in rebuilding Windsor Castle. He was first appointed lord chancellor of England in 1367, the year after he had been appointed to the Winchester see in succession to Bishop Edington.

Throughout his life William of Wickham served as a skilful administrator, a high-ranking 'civil servant'. His enthusiasm for building was apparent during his episcopate. In particular with the help of his master mason or chief architect, William Wynford, he remodelled the cathedral, founded and built Winchester College and repaired the palaces and court houses of the diocese. He also completed the church at St Cross Hospital and founded New College, Oxford.

During his episcopate he continued to serve the King and in 1389 was made lord chancellor for a second time.

1869–73), son of the anti-slave campaigner. The entrance to the famous library of the cathedral leads from the transept. Its greatest treasure is the celebrated 12th-century Winchester Bible, a priceless example of the illuminated texts produced in the cathedral *scriptorium*.

In the south aisle of the cathedral stand the chantries of William Edington (bishop 1345–66) and his famous successor, William of Wickham. Together, these two men made the cathedral one of the great masterpieces of medieval English Gothic architecture. With the wealth that came from his position, William of Wickham founded New College, Oxford, and Winchester College, which became the model for the English public school.

Winchester College is reached from the south-west corner of the cathedral, via a path that leads through the close, which looks private but isn't. The route crosses the garth of the former priory cloisters, of which only three arches remain, on the east side. Through the arches, which once led to the chapter house, can be seen 1 The Close, the official residence of the suffragan bishop of Basingstoke. To the south is the deanery (formerly the prior's hall), which is not generally open to the public. Further south again, across a small green, are the premises of Pilgrims' School, a prep school founded in 1931. At the north end is the Pilgrims' Hall, which is open to the public when not in use. It is a remarkable building dating from about 1295, and has the oldest known hammer-beam roof in the country.

Facing the deanery, near the gateway at the south side of the close, is Cheyney Court. Here the bishop once held his court for the eastern part of the city, which is called the Soke. Outside the gateway is King's Gate, one of the ancient entrances into the medieval walled city. It contains two tiny buildings, namely the chapel of St Swithun-upon-Kingsgate, and a bookshop that specialises in books and prints

on Hampshire. The latter is owned by P & G
Wells, booksellers extraordinary, whose main
shop is nearby in College Street. To the east of
the main shop is the house where, as a plaque
confirms, Jane Austen lived in Winchester
during her final months.

Hereabouts is college territory –
schoolrooms, dormitories, labs, sports facilities
and 'houses'. Also what is virtually the college
pub, the Wykeham Arms, complete with
ancient desks. In 1988 it was chosen as Egon
Ronay Pub of the Year. The official residence of
the headmaster of Winchester College is next
door to Jane Austen's house. Further east is
the porter's lodge and the main entrance to the
college. Regular guided tours start from here in
the summer months. The main layout of the
buildings erected by William of Wickham are
still essentially unchanged, though the college
has greatly expanded its overall extent. The
chapel and, during term time, the cloisters
(where famous Wykehamists are buried) and
Fromond's Chantry are open to the public. So
too is War Cloister, which lies to the west and
is best reached via Commoner's Gate,
Kingsgate Street. It was dedicated in 1924 and
contains memorials to the Wykehamists who
fell in World War I and in all later conflicts.

To the north-east of the college is the palace
of the bishop of Winchester, which is private
and stands alongside the ruins of the medieval
palace, which is open to the public. Called
Wolvesey Palace, it was largely the creation of
the most powerful of all the bishops of
Winchester, Henry of Blois (bishop 1129–74), a
grandson of William I.

Here the trail divides: to the south there is
an extremely pleasant walk across the water
meadows to the Hospital of St Cross, whilst
further east the path curls around the line of
the old city wall and runs alongside the river to
the 'bottom' end of town. We shall describe
first the medieval hospital, which has kept in

Bishop's palace

St Giles's Fair, Winchester
One of the important functions of the medieval church was to organise fairs. 'Church ales' were regularly held to enliven the neighbourhood and fill the church coffers (the predecessor of today's church fête).

The fair at Winchester, which had first been granted to the bishop by William II, was such an important event that legal business closed down in London. It was akin to a modern international trade fair, for merchants came from the length and breadth of the country and also from the Continent. The site of the fair, on St Giles's Hill (part of which is now a public park), was laid out in streets, with booths that remained standing from year to year. Merchants from similar regions and in similar trades were grouped together.

For the duration of the fair the city of Winchester and an area of several miles around it were within the jurisdiction of the bishop. This arrangement ensured that all business was transacted on St Giles's Hill, where weights and measures could be policed and fines and tolls exacted. The heart of the fair was the Bishop's Pavilion or Palm Hall, which has given its name to a modern road in this part of Winchester.

St Giles's Fair reached its peak in the 13th century, though it continued to be held until the 19th century.

the headlines by, first, doling out beer and bread to anyone who asks, and second, exhibiting financial corruption (admittedly over a century ago!) The route to St Cross passes the boundary wall of the college and then dog-legs past New Hall and College Mill. It runs south alongside the river for about a mile. *En route* there are good views of the grounds of the college, including the prominent red-brick facade of the science school.

The Hospital of St Cross was originally founded by Bishop Henry of Blois in about 1130, to care for 13 old men. It was refounded more than 300 years later by Bishop Henry Beaufort. It is his tower and his almshouses that now form the bulk of this remarkable survival, which is still occupied by elderly people. The church dates from the original foundation, but it has such a remarkable series of additions that it is virtually a textbook of medieval architecture. There are guided tours of the hospital all the year round, except on Sundays and Christmas Day.

Returning to Wolvesey Palace, the path to the 'bottom' end of town passes some parts of the original city wall erected by the Romans in the early 3rd century AD. The path emerges opposite City Mill, an 18th-century structure now used as a youth hostel. It is also open to the general public. The Printed Page in Bridge Street is a prime target for print collectors.

To the east of City Mill is St Giles's Hill, the site of a great international medieval fair, and an excellent point from which to survey the Winchester landscape. A well-made, but steep path leads up to the summit from the foot of the hill. To the west lie the Broadway and Abbey Gardens and the unmistakable form of King Alfred (848–99). This great man is virtually 'the patron saint' of Winchester. He had his palace here, was buried here, and spent much of his time here, forging a literate and civilised kingdom in the face of Viking threats. During his lifetime, Winchester rose as Southampton fell, to create a 'pecking order' that largely survived until the last century. When he died he left instructions to be buried in a New Minster beside the cathedral. This religious community was later translated to the *Hyde district* of the city. His wife was buried in another new religious house, namely St Mary's Abbey, which gives its name to Abbey Gardens. Traces of St Mary's are displayed beside the path that runs between Abbey Gardens and the Guildhall, which is itself a fairy-tale bit of Victorian Gothic dating mainly from 1873.

The High Street runs from the Guildhall to the West Gate. It is the main shopping centre of the city. There are, however, some shops to be found to the south in the Square, including Gilbert's famous bookshop, whilst a brand-new shopping complex is being built to the north of High Street in an area called the Brooks. A notable feature of High Street is the Pentice, a medieval relic that provides an attractive covered way outside a line of shops. It is amusing to see, from the variety of pillars, the different ways in which architects over the years have interpreted the Classical tradition!

Old Guildhall clock

The West Gate, which contains a small museum, provides a bird's-eye view of Winchester. Near by is the Great Hall, which is one of the treasures of the city. It was built by Henry III in about 1222 within the walls of the great medieval castle that once stood on this side of the city and is a remarkable structure of great elegance. At the east end are a fine set of stainless steel gates that commemorate the wedding of the Prince of Wales and Lady Diana Spencer in 1981. On the south side of the Great Hall is Queen Eleanor's Gardens, a modern re-creation of a medieval garden named after Henry III's wife. The best-known feature of the Great Hall is, however, the round table that hangs on the west wall. Reputed to be the round table at which King Arthur sat with his knights, it has in fact been shown by modern research to be a late 13th-century fake, but a very good fake, of course!

Above the Great Hall, and reached from the Romsey Road, is the Royal Green Jackets Museum, which is currently being entirely reorganised to update the displays. A nearby block will also accommodate the Royal Hussars Museum, which is being removed from elsewhere in Winchester and the Gurkha Museum, which was formerly at Church Crookham, near Aldershot. Both museums are within the Peninsula Barracks, the main block of which originally built as a palace for Charles II, whose plan to bring the court to Winchester died with him in 1685. The Royal Hampshire Regiment Museum lies to the south, in Serle's House, Southgate Street. It tells the story of the county regiment, which was the successor to the long tradition of volunteer corps raised by the gentry.

Ovington church

Winchester's brand-new swimming pool and Riverside Leisure Centre (the previous one was severely damaged by fire) are in the Hyde district of the city to the north. This is a pleasant little suburb with traces of Hyde Abbey (formerly the New Minster). Some even claim with good authority that King Alfred is buried outside the east end of St Bartholomew's church, which stands opposite the gatehouse of the Abbey. The famous Pilgrims' Way, that reputedly ran between Winchester and Canterbury, starts from Hyde. Its first leg is rather confusingly called the Nuns' Walk, and leads alongside the River Itchen to King's Worthy. It starts from the north-west corner of the large recreation ground that surrounds the leisure centre. To the east of the path are the water meadows of Abbot's Barton and Winnall Moors, a large area of unimproved land that is managed as a nature reserve. There is an extremely pleasant walk around a small public section of the reserve, which can be reached from the north-east corner of the recreation field. Fly fishermen may have heard of the Abbot's Barton stretch of the Itchen from the writings of G E M Skues.

King's Worthy (which includes Abbot's Worthy in its parish) is one of the four Worthys that are strung along the upper valley of the Itchen. Lord Eversley (1831–1928), the Liberal cabinet minister and champion of common rights, retired to Abbot's Worthy House. **Headbourne Worthy** has a celebrated Saxon church with the hacked-off traces of what was once a splendid rood.

It is possible to walk almost the whole way between Winchester and Alresford via public footpaths, starting from the Nuns' Walk. Despite the presence of the M3, which was thrown across the valley in 1985, such places as Easton, Itchen Abbas, Avington, Lovington, Ovington and Itchen Stoke have a timeless charm. There is a cricket green at **Easton** and the church has a remarkable monument to Agatha Barlow (died 1568), who had five daughters, each of whom married a bishop.

Charles Kingsley wrote part of the *Water Babies* in the Plough Inn at Itchen Abbas. **Avington** has a famous fishery and one of the finest country parks in the county. Its sheep-nibbled picnic site runs down to the edge of Avington Pond, a much-silted expanse of water in front of Avington House. This stately pile, where Charles II dallied with Nell Gwyn, is open to the public. It is worth seeing just for its orangeries. Near by is a wholly Georgian church, complete with box pews and all the trappings of squirearchy.

A delightful small road runs along the south bank of the river, between Avington and Ovington. There is an extremely pleasant path alongside the river, between the Bush Inn at Ovington – itself a legendary pub – and **Itchen**

Fishing the Itchen
The Test and Itchen are rivers which are known throughout the world. They both have runs of salmon but it is mainly the trout that brings fishermen from far and wide. At one time these men (and a few ladies) came to pit their wits only against 'brownies', the native trout that grows to prodigious sizes in rich, gin-clear, alkaline waters. But now they are more likely to hook 'rainbows', a species of trout which has been introduced into both the Test and the Itchen.

Fishing on the Hampshire rivers is by 'fly only', even 'dry fly only'. This means that fish can be caught only with an artificial fly, and preferably one that floats. G E M Skues (1858–1949), a famous man in fishing circles, was one of those who challenged the dry-fly dogma by arguing that trout feed naturally on the nymph stage of the life cycle of an aqueous insect. For his pains he was obliged to give up his position in a syndicate on the Itchen above Winchester, where he had fished for more than 50 years.

The hub of Itchen fishing was once a small tackle shop in the Square, Winchester, where Foreign Minister Lord Grey might be found on his way to his fishing cottage at Itchen Abbas. Winchester still is the 'fishing capital' of the Itchen, but the action has moved to the Rod Box, in St George's Street, where a day's fishing might be arranged.

Stoke, whose church stands in redundant splendour on the B3047 Alresford road. It was built in 1866 to resemble La Sainte Chapelle in Paris and is sumptuously finished.

The Itchen above Winchester is one of the finest unspoilt chalk streams in Europe: it supports otters and has a naturally breeding population of brown trout (as well as rainbows). The valley has been carefully preserved by successive land owners, and, apart from the presence of the M3, it has scarcely a trace of industry. Although not quite as pristine, much of the lower valley of the Itchen, below Winchester, is unspoilt, at least as far as the industrial hinterlands of Southampton. The path to St Cross described above continues to Shawford and on to Otterbourne, Brambridge and Bishopstoke. Much of it follows the towpath of the Itchen Navigation, which dates from the late 17th century, long before the heyday of canals dug *de novo*. This ran between Black Bridge Wharf, Winchester (where the college now has its boathouses) and Woodmill, Southampton, though it never made much money.

The village of **Twyford** to the south of Winchester is a place of antique shops and pubs, with its church tucked away in a picturesque backwater beside the river. The church tower rests on twelve 'Druidic stones' that were discovered *in situ* when a former church was dismantled in 1876. Twyford School is a notable local prep school. It was immortalised by a former pupil, Thomas Hughes, in *Tom Brown's Schooldays*.

Facing Twyford, on the opposite bank of the river, is **Shawford**, a popular residential area. To the south is the village of **Otterbourne**, once the home of the novelist Charlotte Yonge (1823–1901), who was extremely popular in her day. Her *Heir of Redclyffe* was reprinted 20 times and was quoted by cabinet ministers. She had a strong

'father/daughter' relationship with John Keble
(1792–1866), a famous Victorian churchman
and a key figure in the Oxford Movement. Her
grave and his memorial stand close together in
the churchyard at Otterbourne. He was vicar of
Hursley near by, where in 1848 he built the
present church, financing the work from
royalties earned with his ecclesiastical
bestseller, *The Christian Year*.

Hursley is now best known as the home of
IBM UK Research Laboratories, where
computer wizards write sophisticated software.
The history of Hursley House, where the firm
has housed its UK research activities since
1958, is of considerable interest, though it is
not ordinarily open to the public. Hursley Park
was originally enjoyed by the bishops of
Winchester. The mutilated ruins of a castle
built in 1138 by Bishop Henry of Blois still
stand in the grounds. The estate was
subsequently held by Richard Cromwell, the
Protector's son, who married the owner's
daughter. It then came into the possession of a
succession of Heathcotes. In 1836, Sir William
Heathcote (1801–81), who had been a pupil of
John Keble's at Oxford, lured the great man to
his living at Hursley. Much later, in 1940,
Hursley House was requisitioned for use by
what became Vickers Supermarine,
manufacturers of the Spitfire, whose works at
Woolston, near Southampton, had been
destroyed by enemy bombing.

A lonely road leads from Otterbourne
across the river to the hamlet of **Brambridge**.
On the way it passes a great avenue of limes,
which were probably planted by an owner of
Brambridge House, Walter Smythe. In 1785,
his twice-widowed daughter, Mrs Fitzherbert,
caused a monumental scandal by secretly
marrying the Prince of Wales, who later
became George IV. The marriage probably took
place at Brambridge House, but it could not be
legalised as she was a Catholic.

One of the most interesting places to visit within easy reach of Winchester is **Marwell Zoological Park**. Started in 1972, it is a new-style zoo that is devoted to preserving endangered species. It has gained an international reputation for such animals as the scimitar-horned oryx, which is close to extinction, and the curiously named Przewalksi horse, which has already been lost in the wild. There are more than 1,000 animals to see at the zoo, including giraffes, wallabies, zebras and 'big cats' – snow leopards, Siberian tigers, servals, cheetahs and Asian lions. It makes a fine day out in a good cause. There are places to picnic, train rides and a 'cuddly animals' farmyard area for young children.

Marwell Hall, a predecessor of the present building, was the home of Henry Seymour, brother of Jane Seymour, whose marriage to Henry VIII is said to have taken place here.

A popular destination with Wintonians is Farley Mount, a strange memorial to a horse. It looks down on Hursley from a high down 4 miles to the west of Winchester and is reached via Sarum Road. From a distance 'the mount' looks like a church spire, but it is in fact the tombstone of a horse that in 1733 leapt into a chalk-pit 25ft deep, with its rider on its back. Both lived to tell the tale.

Farley Mount

The mount has given its name to Farley Mount Country Park, a large expanse of woodland and open downland, with air 'worth sixpence a pint', as Keats once wrote. It is on the route of the Clarendon Way, a long-distance footpath that follows the line of the ridge between Salisbury and Winchester, passing through Pitton, Winterslow, Broughton and King's Somborne. It takes its name from Clarendon Palace, the medieval royal residence that once stood to the east of Salisbury.

An attractive route back to Winchester from Farley Mount takes a road that runs north through Crab Wood to the village of **Sparsholt**.

This contains the famous Lainston House Hotel and also the Hampshire College of Agriculture, which has a notable 'open day' and is the largest college of its kind in the country. Two miles away is **Crawley**, a charming village reached by turning west on the A272 and then north after a mile.

Crawley Court is the home of the engineering branch of the now-threatened Independent Broadcasting Authority, which moved out of London in 1970. Its modern offices occupy the site of a mansion house built originally in 1877 but restored in 1901 by a man who made a fortune from cotton thread. This is Ernest Philippi (1847–1917), who ran J & P Coats of Paisley, near Glasgow. In 1901 he decided to retire to Crawley and keep his reins on the business by means of that relatively new invention, the telephone. It was an early example of an 'electronic office'. His enormous energy spilled over into the village, much of which he bought, cottage by cottage, and then transformed. The mock-Tudor Fox and Hounds pub, and many similar buildings, rose up in place of earth-floored hovels. He subsidised a shop, started a band and built a village hall and a covered skating rink (later burnt down). Orchard Cottages, which are near the pub, still have a Bavarian façade.

Another Crawley relic with a story stands on the left-hand side of the path to the church porch. This is Archdeacon Jacob's Cross, actually an undistinguished-looking post. It once stood between Winchester and Wherwell on the B3420 road, where it meets the Crawley road. Its purpose was to carry a light to guide the Rev Jacobs on his frequent visits to the hamlet of Hunton, which was a chapelry of Crawley. He had the light made after getting totally lost in a snowstorm.

Hunton is one of a string of settlements in the valley of the River Dever, a good trout stream and a modest tributary of the River Test.

Hunton

There is a pretty drive between Sutton Scotney and Micheldever, via Wonston, Hunton, Stoke Charity, Weston Colley and Northbrook. The charming main (and only) street of Hunton once carried the A30 London road, but it was deflected by *force majeure*. It is one of the prettiest streets in the county. A village pump stands in front of the tiny Old School House. The fine manor house dates from the 18th century, but was gentrified in the 1930s and again in about 1950. Opposite is Hunton Down House, a modern building with a very old (Tudor?) flint-and-stone dovecote in its garden. There is a clear view of it from an adjacent footpath.

Stoke Charity church is one of the delights of the Dever Valley. It is basically Norman, with later additions, but no major changes have been made to the fabric since 1250. It has a double squint, one of probably only two in the country, and a rare sculpture of the Mass of St Gregory. This survived the Protestant purges of the reign of Edward VI by being embedded in the wall. It was rediscovered in 1849. Anyone with an interest in heraldry can have a field day in Stoke Charity church: there are well-researched 'crib sheets'.

Micheldever is a large village that stands only a mile to the west of the A33, which was originally a Roman road, turnpiked ca.1760. Micheldever has, however, not been unduly influenced by the traffic near by, now carried by the M3, but has remained a largely agricultural community, with the usual influx of commuters. Micheldever station stands a mile to the north, but it too has had remarkably little effect on the village. The church, the school (with clock tower), the shop, the smithy and the tiny village green (called 'the crease') form an assembly which is now very rare. The church has a remarkably airy octagonal nave, built in 1808 by George Dance for the then new owner, Sir Francis Baring. The church contains some superb monuments to the Barings by the sculptor John Flaxman. In the churchyard is the unmarked grave of Henry Cook, an agricultural labourer hanged after the Swing Riots of 1830, allegedly for knocking off the hat of William Bingham Baring JP of *Northington Grange*. It is said that snow never lies on Henry Cook's grave.

The Barings lived at Stratton House, on the east side of the A33, which is straddled by the twin villages of East and West Stratton, which have been dominated by the successive estate owners. George Dance designed Stratton House in 1803, but only the great portico remains, now standing beside a pond built into a modern private house of 1965. The family links between the Barings of East Stratton and Northington are reflected in the churches of the two places, which are both by Sir Thomas Jackson.

ALRESFORD

New Alresford is a place of unusual pleasures. It has long overtaken Old Alresford as the main settlement on the River Alre, whose copious waters feed the River Itchen. The new town was one of those 'planted' by the bishop of Winchester at the beginning of the 13th century, though in 1689 it was virtually destroyed by fire. Broad Street was purpose-designed for holding markets (its recently revived sheep fair is, however, held elsewhere) and it can still take the paraphernalia of a travelling fair.

Although New Alresford is only a small place, it contains a remarkably large number of pubs, restaurants, and speciality shops. West Street and East Street contain a glass engraver's, fine art dealer's, a fly-fisher's shop, a clockmaker's, antiques shops, some very fine grocers and butchers and much else. Broad Street too has several shops of rare interest, including Laurence Oxley's bookshop and art

Hampshire and the Swing Riots
The most famous of the spontaneous riots that occurred in the last century are those of 1830. They started in Kent in June but quickly spread throughout the southern part of the country. Hampshire was in turmoil from 17 to 26 November. The rioting involved arson, extortion of money, meetings to claim higher wages and bouts of machine-breaking, notably at the Upper Clatford works of the agricultural engineers, Taskers of Andover.

Threatening notes signed 'Captain Swing' were delivered to farmers and others, but no ringleader was ever discovered. Suspicions in Hampshire were levelled at men such as William Cobbett and Henry 'Orator' Hunt MP, but it seems that the riots were genuinely spontaneous protests against the poverty of the times.

With the exception of a few areas, including the New Forest and the north-east corner of the county, the whole of Hampshire experienced some form of unrest in November 1830. Those places which had particularly severe rioting included Fordingbridge, Romsey, Andover, Monk Sherborne, East Woodhay, South Stoneham, Headley and Micheldever. When order was resumed, more than 100 men were transported, many were imprisoned and two were hanged, namely, James Cooper of Fordingbridge and Henry Cook of Micheldever.

Hampshire watercress
The chances are that the watercress you buy in the supermarket was grown in Hampshire, which has become one of the major centres for growing this year-round salad crop. The shallow gravel-bottomed beds where the plant is grown are a familiar sight beside the chalk streams which are its native habitat. However, growing watercress today involves a great deal of technique, including careful selection of the best variety, raising the crop from seed and maintaining a bed which is supplied with a constant stream of clear water at a temperature of 51–2 degrees Fahrenheit. Originally watercress was grown where natural springs welled up, but today most beds are fed by specially drilled artesian wells.

The traditional role of watercress was as a winter salad. The advent of the railway meant that fresh-picked cress could be whisked up to the cities, a trend which later gave the name 'The Watercress Line' to the line from Winchester to Alton via Alresford. In recent years methods of mechanical cultivation and packing have turned a relatively small industry into a full-scale commercial operation. Much of the initiative for these developments came from Hampshire Watercress Limited, a company based at Alresford with extensive beds at Hurstbourne Priors, beside the great viaduct of the railway line between Basingstoke and Andover.

gallery. A plaque on the west side marks the house where the writer Mary Russell Mitford (1787–1855) once lived.

A public footpath runs alongside a stretch of Alresford's river. It starts at the foot of Broad Street, beside the town mill, runs west to the Dean, and thence into West Street. *En route* it passes Alresford Fulling Mill, which dates from the 14th century (though the building is much later). The mill powered wooden mallets that were used for beating the fibres of woven cloth into a tougher felt-like fabric. Until recently it was the home of Mr and Mrs G B Gush, who for many years grew and sold plants for charity, raising over £28,000.

New Alresford was once on a branch railway line that ran from Winchester to London, via Alton and Farnham. It was popularly called the Watercress Line, as its most important function was to move local produce to the London markets. In 1973 this under-used cross-country route was closed between Winchester and Alton, but within four years it had been bought and reopened by steam enthusiasts. The venture has had its financial ups and downs but enthusiasm has triumphed and a largely volunteer force now provides a delightful 'Toytown' service between Alresford and the British Rail station at Alton. A regular schedule operates between the months of March and October, with Santa Specials over Christmas. The Watercress Belle is a wine-and-dine special that operates regularly on Saturdays throughout the season – prebooking essential! Nostalgia on wheels. The main engine shed and yard are at Ropley, and the train also stops at a station at Medstead and Four Marks.

Broad Street, New Alresford, leads past the tiny Victorian fire station to the Soke (relic of the bishop's town) and then across a gigantic medieval causeway that was built to create Alresford Lake. This delightful reed-fringed sheet of water is a refuge for wildfowl. The lake was long believed to have been built to ease navigation of the Itchen, but more plausibly was an episcopal fish pond belonging to the manor of Bishop's Sutton. At the head of the lake is Old Alresford House, which is open to the public. It is reached by turning east at Old Alresford church, signposted to Bighton. The grand house was built by the famous admiral Lord Rodney (1718–92), with prize money won in the 1740s. His career was crowned by defeating the French in 1782 in the West Indies: the cannon he captured in battle still stand outside the house, which offers cream teas and an extensive area of pick-your-own soft fruit.

Old Alresford was where Mary Sumner (1828–1921) founded the Mothers' Union in 1875. She lived with her husband, the rector George Sumner, in Old Alresford Place, which is now a diocesan retreat. The nearby church is Georgian and dates mainly from 1753, though the tower is later. There is a splendid marble monument to Mrs Rodney, who died in 1767 in childbirth. The main village of Old Alresford is north of the church: it has some Victorian estate buildings and a National Children's Home, founded by the Methodist Church.

The B3046 road from Old Alresford to Basingstoke is one of the prettiest routes in Hampshire. It follows the valley of the Candover Stream, where great flocks of Canada geese gather on summer evenings. **Northington Grange** has in recent years been restored and opened to the public. Built in 1809, it is in the form of a Classical temple, though the interior has been gutted. Its great façade, like a British Museum look-alike, stands above a long thin lake and looks across some of the finest country in Hampshire. Go and see it. It was the home of the banker Alexander Baring (1774–1848), who made a fortune in North America, where in 1803 he helped

Mary Sumner (1828–1921)
Mary Sumner founded and built up the Mothers' Union, an organisation which came to represent the interests and needs of millions of women worldwide. The first meetings were held at Old Alresford, where her husband was rector. They were simple affairs at which she realised her idea of 'a union of mothers in prayer for their homes'.

No doubt many a Victorian rector's wife arranged similar events in her husband's parish. But Mary Sumner was fortunate enough to have close links with the bishop of Winchester. In 1885 he recognised the Mothers' Union as a diocesan organisation after Mary Sumner had addressed a mass meeting of women at a Church Congress held at Portsmouth. In the same year her husband was promoted to the Winchester canonry and the couple went to live at 1 The Close, which still stands.

In the following years the Mothers' Union was recognised by many other dioceses, its branches spread to many other countries within the British Empire and it started to publish two very successful periodicals (one edited by Charlotte Yonge). By 1895 it had headquarters in London.

The Mothers' Union has always been a religious organisation and can be criticised for taking a back-seat in the women's rights movement. But Mary Sumner showed that women could run an international organisation.

finance the greatest land deal ever, when the French sold Louisiana (then much larger than the present State) to the Americans. This branch of the family is commemorated in Northington church.

The remains of the church at **Chilton Candover** are often described as an 'underground church'. They are in fact the crypt of the Norman church, forgotten until its rediscovery in 1927.

The countryside to the south of Alresford is of considerable interest. **Tichborne** is famous for its annual dole-out of flour, a practice which dates from the 13th century, when the wife of Sir Roger Tichborne was granted a request to feed the poor from the 23 acres of land that she had managed to crawl around in her dying days. The Tichborne family, who have lived in the village for more than 800 years, came to national prominence in the last century, when Arthur Orton (1834–98), the son of a Wapping butcher, claimed the inheritance by impersonating a long-lost nephew of Sir Henry Tichborne. After a lengthy trial, he was sentenced to 14 years' imprisonment, though, incredibly, his alleged mother continued to believe his story. Tichborne church is full of memorials to various members of the family, who managed after the Reformation to retain a Catholic aisle in an Anglican church.

Further south is the pretty village of **Cheriton**, which gave its name to a famous Civil War battle of 29 March 1644, in which the Royalists were defeated in a six-hour action involving 12,000 men. A monument commemorates the fight, which is re-enacted each year by the English Civil War Society.

A mile to the south of Cheriton, alongside the A272 Petersfield road, is the beautiful estate village of **Hinton Ampner**, much of which was bequeathed to the National Trust by the author Ralph Dutton (1898–1985), 8th Lord Sherborne. After he inherited the estate in 1935 he decided to restore the house to its Georgian splendour. He also redesigned the gardens, a massive task which he made a life's work. They are a masterpiece of intimate landscaping.

BISHOP'S WALTHAM

This small country town stands by itself. It can conveniently be reached from Winchester, either via Colden Common and Lower Upham, or across the downs via Morestead, where the ravages of the great storm of 1987 are particularly evident. As its name suggests, it was once the seat of the bishops of Winchester. The ruins of the palace lie to the south-west of the town centre. The streets of Bishop's Waltham form a rough gridiron pattern and were probably laid out by the bishops. Despite dramatic developments elsewhere in south Hampshire, the town itself has somehow managed to keep its character as a small rural community.

To the east of the main car park is Basinghall Street, which leads past the Barleycorn Inn to the Crown Hotel. This once held Nelson's great rival, the French admiral Villeneuve. He was the most distinguished of the many Frenchmen kept under house arrest in the town (and, indeed, throughout Hampshire) during the Napoleonic Wars. Near the Crown is St George's Square, which once fronted the outer gate of the bishop's palace (it is now separated from the ruins by a modern bypass). Appropriately, the gas-lamp in the centre of the square is topped by a mitre!

A small town museum, open on Sunday afternoons, has recently been opened in Brook Street, which runs off the Square. Of particular interest are the banknotes issued by Gunner's Bank, a local bank founded in 1809 to provide farmers with financial services. It was the last private bank to issue its own banknotes. Other items in the museum include delicate terracotta pottery and 'signed' bricks produced locally at

Bishop Langton's arms, Bishop's Waltham Church

The bishops' palaces
The immense power of the bishops of Winchester was reflected in the large numbers of palaces, or country homes, that they owned. Until 1928 the Diocese of Winchester included the county of Surrey and present Diocese of Portsmouth. The remains of a substantial palace held by the bishops of Winchester still stand in London, alongside Southwark Cathedral, whilst Farnham Castle was for many years the prime seat of the bishop. It returned to Wolvesey Palace, Winchester, only in 1928.

In addition to the palaces at Wolvesey and Bishop's Waltham, there were seven other episcopal seats in Hampshire, namely at Highclere, Bishop's Sutton, Merdon Castle (near Hursley), Marwell, East Meon, Hambledon and Bitterne. With the possible exception of Merdon, which was a refuge, these grand residences were built as places where the bishop or his officers could stay during visits to attend to estate business.

The most durable relics of the palaces are the ponds which held the bishops' fish, notably Alresford Pond (Bishop's Sutton), Fishers Pond (Marwell) and the pond at Bishop's Waltham.

Newtown. The works were originally founded in the early 1860s by Arthur (later Sir Arthur) Helps (1813–75), Queen Victoria's secretary, who had discovered a vein of clay on his estate. Small hard bricks were a speciality; London's Blackfriars Bridge was built with them.

At the north end of Brook Street is the Old Granary, which has an excellent restaurant. Upstairs in a faintly 1960s atmosphere, a colony of artists work at pottery, painting, wood-turning, macramé and much else.

Bank Street runs east from the Old Granary and is said to take its name from Gunner's Bank, which once occupied the yellow-brick premises of the Droxford Registration District. The parish church also stands on this side of town, at the end of St Peter's Street, a delightful curving cul-de-sac. However, with the exception of the coat-of-arms of Bishop Thomas Langton (bishop 1493–1501), which is displayed on the west wall, the church has no trace of the many bishops who stayed at the palace. Above Langton's arms are Cromwellian cannon balls from the Civil War, during which the palace was destroyed. At the west end of the nave is a rare relic, a private pew – in fact a whole gallery of private pews. These were built in 1733 for five parishioners, whose rights to occupy the seats are still attached to their respective houses.

As benefits a place that has been home for many naval men, Bishop's Waltham's church has an Admiral's Corner, including a memorial to Viscount Cunningham, the man who in 1952 donated the site of Bishop's Waltham Palace to the nation. Now managed by English Heritage, it is well worth a visit.

Bishop's Waltham is surrounded by pleasant countryside, including the villages of Durley, Swanmore, Shedfield and Upham. The Brushmakers' Arms, Upham (not to be confused with *Lower* Upham) takes its name from an old village industry.

2 Portsmouth and East Hampshire

This corner of the county has so much to offer that the visitor can be kept busy for a week or more.

The area stretches from the West Sussex border, on one side, to the valley of the Meon on the other. Behind the hump of Portsdown Hill, and to the side of the A3 corridor, it includes some of the finest unspoilt countryside in Hampshire. Villages such as South Boarhunt, Hambledon, Chalton, Buriton, Soberton and East Meon, to name but a few, are a delight. It is a great surprise to find them so close to the hectic towniness of Portsmouth. But the city is largely confined to Portsea Island, with a northerly tail that stretches along the route of the former Portsmouth to Horndean Light Railway.

The area around Butser Hill, near Petersfield, is particularly beautiful. Although its rolling wooded hills were afforested in modern times, they give some idea of what it must have been like when the Forest of Bere spread over most of the district.

Petersfield itself is an attractive small town that grew up alongside the busy London–Portsmouth road. It stands on the south-western edge of the sandy Wealden Beds, which give the area to the north of the town a character of its own. The steep slopes, hollow ways and wooded hangers hereabouts are superb country for walking and exploring. They have inspired many, including the poet Edward Thomas, the naturalist Gilbert White, the actor Sir Alec Guinness and the craftsmen Edward Barnsley.

The City of Portsmouth, with its satellite towns of Gosport, Fareham and Havant, is a gutsy place – not unlike the East End. It is the only place in Hampshire where part of the run

Portsmouth and Southsea

Population: 179,419

Early Closing: Wed

Market Days: Thu, Fri, Sat

Cashpoints: *Barclays* 107 Commerical Rd, 3 Guildhall Walk; *Lloyds* 115 Commerical Rd, 16A High St Cosham, 38 London Rd North End, 6 Clarendon Rd; *Midland* 118 Commerical Rd, 18 London Rd North End, 106 Albert Rd; *Natwest* 130 Commercial Rd, 8 London Rd North End, 71 Osborne Rd, 68 Palmerston Rd

Tourist Information: The Hard, Rudmore Roundabout, Pyramids Centre

Attractions: Charles Dickens' Birthplace Museum*, City Museum and Art Gallery, Cumberland House Natural Science Museum and Butterfly House, D-Day Museum and Overlord Embroidery, Eastney Pumping Station*, Fort Widley*, HMS Victory, HMS Warrior, Mary Rose, Round Tower, Royal Naval Museum, Southsea Castle and Museum, Sea-Life Centre

Arts: Kings Theatre – Portsmouth Players

Leisure: Mountbatten Centre, Pyramids Centre, Victoria Swimming Centre, Wimbledon Park Sports Centre

Cinemas: Cannon, Odeon Film Centre

By Road: London 74 miles

continues overleaf

**Portsmouth and Southsea,
continued**

(A3), Southampton 19 miles
(M27, A3205)

By Rail: 1hr 40mins from
London (Waterloo to
Portsmouth Harbour line).
Direct services to Brighton,
Chichester, Eastleigh,
Havant, Southampton and
Worthing.

By Sea: Scheduled ferry
services to the Isle of Wight
and France

of some national newspapers is printed, at the
News Centre, Hilsea.

The casual visitor to Portsmouth is likely to
get sucked into the great tourist machine – the
preserved ships, the 'naval heritage', the
Palmerston forts, the numerous museums of
the city and so forth. These are of immense
interest, both locally and nationally, but it
would be a pity not to sample some of the
ordinary pubby street life of the place; or to
explore the chic, rather self-conscious streets
and shops of Southsea; or just to sit on the
beach and stare. There is a small patch of beach
at Old Portsmouth, tucked between the Round
Tower and the Square Tower, and as much as
you like between here and Eastney. The best
beaches elsewhere in the area are at Stokes Bay
and Lee-on-Solent, on the Gosport side of the
harbour, and at South Hayling, near Havant. If
you fancy a trip by boat or hovercraft, a long
afternoon on the Isle of Wight is quite feasible.
Southsea still provides traditional seaside fun,
together with the newer delights of the Sea-
Life Centre and the Pyramids Centre, which is
a souped-up fun version of the traditional
winter gardens.

Yachtsmen will have their own sources of
specialist information, but it should be said
that one effect of recent reductions in the naval
presence at Portsmouth is that the harbour has
become a rapidly growing centre for leisure
boating. The new Port Solent Marina Village at
South Lockside is a huge new development,
where residents can tie up 'at the foot of the
garden'.

The serious-minded visitor could easily
spend a week exploring the museums of
Portsmouth and district. Another week would
be needed to visit the surroundings, including
Portchester Castle, the best-preserved Roman
(and medieval) castle in northern Europe,
Butser Ancient Farm, Titchfield Abbey and
much else.

HMS Warrior

PORTSMOUTH AND SOUTHSEA

The City of Portsmouth is not the capital of Hampshire but it is its 'bright lights'. Much of the city's character is due to the fact that it is squashed up on an island two miles by four. Portsmouth has for centuries been the naval outport of London. The Royal Navy created it and until recently sustained it.

All that has now changed. Portsmouth Dockyard, which is now called HM Royal Naval Base, is no longer a major centre for refitting ships but is instead a repair depot and tourist attraction. The city is no longer an exclusively naval city, but is now a centre for a wide range of businesses, including IBM and Zurich Insurance. However, the sight of the Fleet sailing for the South Atlantic in 1982, and the casualties suffered locally, were a reminder that the fates of Portsmouth and the Royal Navy are still intimately entwined.

In recent years the tourist attractions of Portsmouth have grown so rapidly that the visitor now risks fatigue and mental indigestion. There is much to be said for tackling the city in several forays . . . commando-style! Portsmouth's overwhelming theme of war may not be to everybody's taste, but there is great deal of social and national history to be found amidst the gore.

Many visitors come to Portsmouth to take its hovercraft to Ryde, or its ferries to France and the Isle of Wight. Whilst they are here, they may find it convenient to see some parts of the city before sailing, such as the Charles Dickens Birthplace Museum, which is only a short walk from the Continental ferry port at the Albert Johnson Quay.

The major areas of interest in the city are the HM Naval Base, Old Portsmouth, Southsea and Eastney, and Guildhall Square and its environs.

HM Naval Base, or the dockyard, which lies to the north of the cross-harbour ferry

Portsmouth and the South Atlantic campaign

The HM Naval Base at Portsmouth played a critical role in the reclamation of the Falkland Islands from Argentinian forces in 1982. It was from here that the task force set sail and it was also in the Portsmouth area that so many families had to bear sad news in the following months. In early April the local newspaper was headlined 'Fighting fit' and 'Bless 'em all', but a month later, after the sinking of the Type-42 destroyer HMS *Sheffield*, it was reporting 'City of anguish'.

When the ships left they were cheered on their way by huge crowds standing, as is the tradition, on the fortifications of Old Portsmouth. At the centre of the Falklands operations was the aircraft carrier HMS *Hermes*, which, despite many attempts, could not be sunk by the Argentinians. The ship returned to a hero's welcome from Prime Minister Margaret Thatcher and many others at Portsmouth on 21 July 1982.

Royal Marines were deeply involved in the conflict, as detailed in their museum at Eastney. One memorable operation involved the famous 'Great Yomp' across 20 miles of hard mountainous terrain, each man carrying a load equivalent to the weight of a young man.

At Old Portsmouth stands a memorial to the members of the Royal Navy, Royal Marines, Royal Fleet Auxiliary and Merchant Navy who died in the campaign.

The Discovery of the *Mary Rose*

Attempts to salvage the *Mary Rose* after her catastrophic sinking in 1545 started almost immediately. Venetian sailors tried to raise her by attaching hawsers at low tide to two empty vessels held alongside and allowing the tide to lift the wreck. Then in 1836 two pioneer divers, John and Charles Deane, rediscovered the *Mary Rose*, quite by chance, when they were called to check an obstruction fouling fishermen's nets.

Fortunately, somebody marked the position of the wreck with a red cross on an obscure chart which was lodged in the RN Hydrographers' Department. This was later discovered by Alexander McKee, journalist and amateur sub-aqua diver, who in 1965 had started to look for wrecks in the Solent. It showed that the wreck of the *Mary Rose* was quite close to Southsea Castle.

However, even though sonar tracings revealed anomalies in the sea-bed close to the expected site of the vessel, it was not until 1971 that Percy Ackland, first discovered tangible evidence of the ship in the form of planking sticking up from the bed of the sea.

In the following years, the raising of the *Mary Rose* became a great national cause, but it was not until 1982 that archaeologist Margaret Rule decided that her team had carried out sufficient undersea excavation to allow the old timbers to be lifted.

terminus, is the focus of everything that has happened in Portsmouth since 1495, when Henry VII ordered the building of the first-known dry dock in the country. The ability to haul great ships out of the water and do things to them in quiet water has always been vital to the Navy. With the Isle of Wight acting as a great breakwater, and France within a day's sailing, Portsmouth was the natural choice for the site of the premier naval port on the south coast. These factors, and the deep channel at the mouth of Portsmouth Harbour, which is scoured twice daily by 'four square miles' of water, fixed the fate of Portsea Island.

Visitors can freely enter a small part of the dockyard, but the Falklands Campaign of 1982 showed that this is still a working base and may be shut at times of national emergency. The most prominent feature of the yard is the lofty Semaphore Tower, with its ship-like mast and rigging. It is the nerve centre of the Commander-in-Chief Portsmouth. Many of the other buildings are of historic interest and date from the latter half of the 18th century.

It is, of course, the ships preserved at Portsmouth that are of most general interest. Although it is tempting to start with HMS *Warrior*, which lies beside the main gate of the dockyard, she is in fact the youngest vessel on display and it is more logical to start with the *Mary Rose*, and then proceed to HMS *Victory* near by, before returning to the *Warrior*. After that, the galleries of the Royal Naval Museum will easily fill an hour or two and are essential browsing for those with a serious interest in naval history.

The *Mary Rose* is probably the most remarkable ship in the world. Not only was she lost in the most remarkable way, in Spithead within sight of Henry VIII, but she was recovered by inspired treasure-hunting (and 17 years' hard graft).

The remains of the Tudor ship include most

of the starboard side and now stand upright in the Ship Hall, where the old timbers are continuously kept cool and wet to minimise rot and prevent drying out. A selection of the 14,000 artefacts found in the wreck are on display in a nearby Georgian boathouse.

A tour of HMS *Victory* is almost an exercise in naval PR, which is perhaps appropriate for the flagship of the Commander-in-Chief Naval Home Command. But the opportunity to look round this fine 'first-rate' warship, Nelson's flagship, should not be missed. Although *Victory's* hour of glory was the battle of Trafalgar in 1805, she had already been afloat for almost 50 years and was to stay in the water until 1920, when she was rescued and restored to her present position. The work continues, with the aim of restoring her to her 1805 state by the late 1990s.

Ships like the *Victory* were made obsolescent by ships like the *Warrior*, which was launched on the Thames in 1860. This iron-clad, screw-propelled vessel, which also had the option to run under sail, probably represented the most important technical development in naval warfare since the invention of gunpowder.

Warrior is not only a ship of great intrinsic interest; she is also a tribute to the skills of the men of Hartlepool, where she was recently restored – virtually rebuilt. As a transitional ship she had a movable funnel and screw. Hence the order: 'Up funnel! Down screw!'

The work of the generations of Portsmouth men who have built and repaired naval vessels is celebrated in the Museum of the Dockyard Apprentice, which is in the Unicorn Training Centre, reached via Market Way, to the north-east of the dockyard main gate.

Old Portsmouth lies to the south of the dockyard and is within easy walking distance. It is the site of the medieval town of Portsmouth that grew up around an inlet called

HMS *Warrior*
This fine ship was launched in response to the building by the French of the *Gloire*, the first naval ship to be constructed with a wooden hull clad in iron. The two vessels entered the water within four months of each other. They represented the first acceptance by naval commanders that the age of 'wooden walls' was over. When the *Warrior* was launched, iron-hulled merchant ships had been known for 40 years: the SS *Great Britain* had shown for almost 20 years that a screw-driven iron ship could cross the Atlantic.

The engines of the *Warrior* were a novelty in the Navy (and a messy one!). They consumed about 12 tons of coal per hour, which meant that the 850 tons which could be stowed gave the ship a range of about 1,000 miles.

Perhaps the most remarkable outcome of the advent of the *Warrior*, which never fired a shot in anger, is that she set off a Victorian arms race in which bigger and better guns were matched by ships with more and more armour. Within a few years she had herself become obsolete, outclassed by later developments. In terms of ship design, she was the most important vessel to be launched until 1906, when HMS *Dreadnought* slid into the water at Portsmouth. This ship had been built to match a threat from a new enemy, Germany.

the Camber. Here in about 1188 a church was founded by a merchant, John of Gisors. For nearly 800 years it remained a parish church, but in 1927, the year after Portsmouth officially became a city, it became the cathedral of the newly created Anglican Diocese of Portsmouth.

The Camber, overlooked by its church, is still a small commerical port and is also the terminus of the Isle of Wight car ferry. This part of Portsmouth was once called Spice Island, on account of its numerous pubs and bordellos. It is an enchanting place to while away a summer's evening, watching the ships.

Portsmouth Cathedral is unfinished. Plans to extend the medieval church to the west were cut short by the last war and are only beginning to be reactivated. Inevitably, the siting of the tower of the old church in the middle of the building means that it will always be a jungle of pillars and archways.

The cathedral is entered from the south porch. Immediately on the right is the Golden Barque, the former weather vane of the church. Touching it is said to make sailors undrownable. Halfway along the south aisle is a large slate slab commemorating the final resting-place in 1984 of an Unknown Sailor from the *Mary Rose*, from which many human bones were recovered. On the south side of the chancel, which is the oldest part of the church, is the Buckingham Monument. Buckingham, who was a favourite of Charles I, was killed at 11 High Street in 1628. Another notorious local killing was that of the bishop of Chichester in 1450, who was lynched outside the *Domus Dei*, the garrison church. The ruins of this medieval church still stand, beside the cobbled square of Grand Parade, at the foot of the High Street. It lost the roof of its nave in the blitz and has never been repaired. It was here that Charles II married Catherine of Braganza in 1662.

The High Street, Old Portsmouth, was where many naval officers lodged before

Portsmouth Cathedral

boarding ship via the sallyport alongside the Square Tower. In 1787 some of them joined HMS *Sirius* and the other ships of the First Fleet, bound for Botany Bay, Australia. A memorial beside the Square Tower commemorates this epic voyage.

It is a breezy walk of a mile or more from Old Portsmouth to **Southsea**. This is the posh end of town, which started to grow up in 1810–20 behind the large common to the east of Old Portsmouth, particularly during 1837–60. The prime mover was a local architect-cum-speculator, Thomas Owen (1804–62). The focus of the area, which makes pleasant walking for Victoriana buffs, is St Jude's church of 1851. Arthur Conan Doyle, creator of Sherlock Holmes, lived in Southsea between 1882 and 1890. The site of his house, 1 Bush Villas, Elm Grove, is marked by a plaque.

The social life of Southsea in the early 1800s revolved around the pump-room and other facilities provided in the vicinity of what is now Clarence Pier, which came later. The building of South Parade Pier in 1908–9 firmly established Southsea's place as a resort. Such essentials of the inter-wars resort as a floral clock, rock-strewn gardens, and a canoe lake are still there, almost as period pieces. Today the main attractions, however, are the D-Day Museum, the Sea-Life Centre, the Pyramids Leisure Centre and to a lesser extent the Natural Science Museum at Cumberland House and the Royal Marines Museum at Eastney.

The D-Day Museum was hastily built in 1984 to commemorate the 40th anniversary of the Allied invasion of Europe, which was masterminded from Southwick House, near Portsmouth. The bravery of the troops, the ingenuity of the engineers and the logistical feats of the planners still amaze. This pivotal event of the last war comes alive in a very entertaining way.

Conan Doyle in Southsea
The young doctor who came to Southsea in June 1882 apparently decided to settle here merely because it was served by a steamer from Plymouth. He had had an unhappy first experience of medical practice in the Devon town, where he had worked with another doctor whose habits he regarded as unethical. He was luckier in Southsea and managed to build up a comfortable practice as a sole GP.

It was during his time at Southsea that he started to write short stories and articles and, in particular, devised the characters of Sherlock Holmes and Dr Watson. There seems little doubt that some of his ideas, and even perhaps the character of Dr Watson, came from his membership of the Portsmouth Literary and Scientific Society. He was also a keen player-member of the Portsmouth Cricket Club and a founder member and a keen player (for some reason under an assumed name!) of the Portsmouth Football Club.

In 1890, by now a married man, he left Southsea with little idea of what he wanted to do. There followed an abortive trip to Berlin to investigate a 'cure' for tuberculosis and an equally futile attempt to set up as an eye specialist in Harley Street. Thereafter, he lived the life of a writer, but he never forgot Hampshire. In later years he returned to live at Minstead in the New Forest.

The parallels with the Norman Invasion, which of course went the other way, are emphasised by the museum's equivalent to the Bayeux Tapestry, namely the Overlord Embroidery, 272ft long, which was commissioned from the Royal School of Needlework by Lord Dulverton long before the museum was conceived. It is a beautiful and moving piece of work.

The importance of South Hampshire in the defence of the realm is emphasised by the surviving Tudor castle that stands to the south of the D-Day Museum. This was part of the string of forts that were built by Henry VIII to defend the whole of the English coast. It was from here in 1545 that he watched the *Mary Rose* sink to the bottom of Spithead.

The castle itself, with its arrow-shaped bastions, is of great interest, but it also contains an exhibition which tells the story of the defences of what became Fortress Portsmouth. The way in which developments in offensive weapons led to the need for better defences is fascinating, and explains the ever-increasing rings of ramparts that encircled Portsmouth Harbour. All these were made obsolete by the invention of the aeroplane, as Portsmouth discovered to its great cost during the blitz.

On a lighter note, two of the most popular modern attractions on the Southsea seafront are the huge blue-glass Pyramids Leisure Centre, where children (and adults) can have the time of their life in a tropical micro-climate, and the Sea-Life Centre, where they can find (and touch!) what they can't find on the beach.

The east end of Southsea shades into Eastney, which has long been the home of the marines. The barracks were run down in 1972, when the Royal Marines Museum was expanded and housed in the splendid former officers' mess.

The special role of the marines, ie as soldiers trained to fight from a ship base, can

Charles Dickens Birthplace Museum

be traced back to 1644, though there was no established force until 1755. In 1982 more than half of the entire corps was sent to the South Atlantic to fight in the Falklands. The succession of campaigns on display in the museum is rather numbing, but the work of the marines is interesting.

The municipal centre of Portsmouth is the Guildhall Square, where the ornate grandeur of the Guildhall of 1890 (rebuilt after the blitz) is nicely offset by modern black-glass offices.

The 'New' Theatre Royal of 1884 to the south of the Guildhall no longer puts on productions, but has been conserved and now forms a classy place to take a drink and a snack. From the north of the square runs the main shopping centre of the city. There is a preponderance of chain stores; specialist shopping is best done at Southsea.

For the sports enthusiast there is first-class soccer at Fratton Park and international athletics (and much else) at the superb new Mountbatten Centre.

Old Portsmouth

From the centre of Portsmouth the M275 leads across the reclaimed lands of Horsea 'Island' to meet the M27. Almost immediately a turning from the intricate Junction 12 leads to the A27 and **Portchester**. This is the site of the earliest port in the harbour, founded by the Romans and used actively throughout the medieval period. Much of the old castle has survived and is well worth visiting. From the top of the great keep there is a fine view of the harbour. Southwick Priory was founded at Portchester and its monks built the 12th-century church which stills stands within the outer bailey of the castle.

A country road climbs up from Portchester to the top of **Portsdown Hill**, where a monument to Lord Nelson stands alongside Fort Nelson. This is one of the four Palmerston forts open to the public, the others being Fort Widley, three miles to the east, Fort

Brockhurst, Gosport, and the sea-girt Spit Bank Fort. They are not pretty but they recall a fascinating period of English military history. The advent of rifled guns of great range in the 1860s meant that the city and dockyard needed to be protected from an encircling action, whereby an enemy could fire effectively from Portsdown Hill.

A highlight of the tours of Forts Nelson and Widley is the chance to walk through galleries dug in the chalk by Welsh miners. Here were kept the powder and shells that just might have been needed if some foreign power had tried to take Portsmouth.

Guns on loan from the Royal Armoury in the Tower of London are on display at Fort Nelson. The view from the top of Fort Widley across the harbour is one of the finest in England. Whiling away an hour parked on the hill is a local sport . . . night and day.

Southwick is scarcely two miles to the north of Fort Widley, and yet it is a rural village through and through. In fact, with the exception of Southwick House, it is wholly owned by a local landowner, whose estate covers 7,000 acres. It grew up around the priory originally founded at Portchester, but virtually nothing remains of the priory buildings, which fell into lay hands at the Dissolution.

Southwick House is famous as the place from which General Eisenhower and his staff commanded the D-Day invasions of Normandy in 1944. The operations board they used still hangs in the wardroom of HMS *Dryad*, the naval establishment that now occupies the house.

Southwick still has its own local brewhouse, albeit in mothballs. It stands behind the Golden Lion pub and has survived almost untouched from the days when 'Hunt's Home-Brewed Ales' were brewed there, for the pub itself and one outlet in Portsmouth. The brewhouse, which was restored with a one-off celebration brew-up in 1985, can be viewed by appointment.

South Boarhunt is owned by the same landowner as Southwick, and it too is a place that seems to have been overlooked by the 20th century. It consists of little more than a farm, a pond and a church. Prominent in the latter is the spacious boxed squire's pew, which is still regularly used. The church is a fine example of a building that is essentially Saxon, although it has been lengthened westwards. It was built just before the Norman Conquest and still shows several original features, such as the window in the north wall of the chancel and the chancel arch. A Saxon door is obscured by a monument to Robert Eddowes, who was a 'storekeeper of ordnance' at Portsmouth in the years before this sensitive facility was moved to the quiet shores of Priddy's Hard, Gosport. A 1914–18 memorial to the aptly named Sergeant-Pilot Arthur Wing is a reminder that flying was not always the prerogative of officers.

The countryside to the north of Portsmouth is full of surprises. At **Denmead** is a large industrial pottery with family facilities and a reject pottery showroom for bargain hunters. Nearby **Catherington** is close enough to the city to have long been a favourite with senior naval officers, yet it is pleasantly tucked away in open countryside. It is the mother parish of Horndean, which has now overtaken it.

Catherington church and its interesting overgrown churchyard are well worth a visit. On the north side of the nave is a rare medieval wall painting, showing St Michael weighing souls on a balance, with a demon pushing down at one end and the Virgin Mary at the other.

The splendid tomb of Sir Nicholas Hyde (d.1631) and his wife is another of the church's treasures. It stands amidst lumber in a chapel on the north side of the chancel. He was a famous judge and also lord of the nearby manor of Hinton Daubnay. Brightly painted effigies of the couple lie beneath an ornate canopy, with their 10 children in front.

Outside the east end of the church stands the tomb of two Thespians, Charles and Ellen Kean. His father was Edmund Kean, the great Shakespearian tragedian, who once lived at Keydell House, Catherington.

Near by under trees is the tomb of Admiral Sir Charles Napier (1786–1860), a colourful naval adventurer who lived at Horndean. His dress was extraordinary: as well as wearing a smock, to curry favour with the locals, he had 'a superfluity of shirt collar and small neck-handkerchief, always bedaubed with snuff . . . trousers far too short and . . . the ugliest pair of old shoes'! Another admiral who lived at Catherington was Lord Hood (1724–1816), friend of Nelson, whose fine 18th-century house at the corner of Five Heads Road is now a retreat for the Diocese of Portsmouth.

A rare man-operated tread-wheel that was until recently used to raise water at Kinch's Farm, Catherington, now has pride of place at the Weald and Downland Open-Air Museum, near Chichester.

Hambledon is a village that is so often credited with the birth of cricket that the village itself is overlooked. Yet it is one of the most

Bat and Ball Inn, Hambledon

charming places in Hampshire and stands on the edge of a large AONB (area of outstanding natural beauty). A peep inside the parish church (which contains a Saxon structure) is enough to show that in the Middle Ages it was a thriving community of considerable wealth. It was granted the usual rights to a market and a fair and still had a market hall as late as 1819, when the trade had long gone. This stood in the short wide High Street that leads up to the church.

Hambledon today is renowned for its fine English wine, which comes from a vineyard to the north-east of the church. This was started in 1951, almost as a hobby, by General Sir Guy Salisbury-Jones, who is credited with having revived the English wine business. A footpath, one of 50 in the area, leads from the churchyard and gives a good view of the long lines of vines. The path leads on to Ridge Meadow, the Hambledon Cricket Club's present ground, which is sponsored by Hartridge Soft Drinks, a long-established local business, founded in 1882. This is the third ground to be used by the club. The Bat and Ball Inn and a huge ugly granite obelisk now commemorate the momentous events that took place here between about 1750 and 1787. In spirit, the matches were akin to the horse-races that were then held on the downs.

FAREHAM

The uppermost reaches of Portsmouth Harbour are the muddy shores of Fareham Creek, too tortuous for it ever to have been a sizeable port. The final twisting mile or two is the tidal estuary of the Wallington River, a modest stream which rises in the Forest of Bere and runs behind the hump of Portsdown Hill, via Southwick and Boarhunt.

Fareham has a waterfront and was once a port of local importance, but it is today a town

Hambledon vineyard
The current resurgence of the English wine industry (there are now nearly a dozen vineyards in Hampshire alone) is due almost entirely to the enthusiasm of one man who in 1951 decided to plant a vineyard at Hambledon. This was Sir Guy Salisbury-Jones (1896–1985), a military man who once said that his interest in viniculture came from his experiences in 1917, when French troops shared their wine with the English.

Sir Guy reasoned that the Hampshire chalk soils were little different from those of the Champagne areas of France and so he decided to produce a dry white wine. The 4,000 vines he selected for planting were mainly from a hybrid stock called Sevre-Villard (now called Seyval), but he also planted a few of the great Chardonnay and Pinot Noir vines (the vines now also include Pinot Meunier and Auxerrois). The resulting wine was compared to those of the Moselle and Alsace regions of Germany, though recent wines are more like the still wines of the Champagne district.

The new owner of the Hambledon Vineyard has doubled its extent to 15 acres. Its annual output has been as high as 25,000 bottles (in 1976) and as low as 400. Visitors can buy direct from the vineyard.

Fareham

Population: 88,609

Early Closing: Wed

Market Day: Mon

Cashpoints: *Barclays* 67/69 West St; *Lloyds* 43 West St; *Midland* 71 West St; *NatWest* 52 West St

Tourist Information: Ferneham Hall, Osborn Rd

Attraction: Portchester Castle (off A27 at Porchester)

Arts: Fareham and Gosport Drama Centre, Ferneham Hall

Leisure: Fareham Leisure Centre

By Road: London 76 miles (M27, A3), Southampton 12 miles (M27), Portsmouth 8 miles (M27)

By Rail: 2hrs from London (branch of the Waterloo to Weymouth line via Eastleigh). Direct services to Eastleigh, Havant, Portsmouth and Southampton

which thrives because it is on the M27 and only a few miles from both Portsmouth and Southampton. Although it has always to some extent prospered as part of the naval hinterland of Portsmouth, it is not as salty as neighbouring Gosport and its charming old High Street shows that it was once rather like Botley or Bishop's Waltham. Bricks and chimney-pots were a major product and 'Fareham reds' can be found in many buildings locally and much further afield (and in Portsmouth City Museum).

Fareham is about to acquire its own museum, which will be housed in Westbury Manor.

Although there are some points of interest for the enthusiast in Fareham itself (such as the remains of the Palmerston forts and the ruins of Cams Hall), the town's main value is as a convenient centre with easy access to a variety of places of interest near by. It is well provided with all mod cons, including a swimming pool and leisure complex, an arts centre (Ferneham Hall) and a large under-cover shopping mall (at the east end of West Street).

It is difficult to believe that the busy town of Fareham was once overshadowed by **Titchfield**, the village which lies immediately to the west. The main reason for this was that the church estates of Titchfield were huge; they extended along the Solent shore, from the Hamble River to Gilkicker Point. The importance of Titchfield depended on the existence of Titchfield Abbey, the remains of which stand on the other side of the A27, some distance to the north of the village. But even before the foundation of the abbey there was a minster church of considerable influence at Titchfield. The porch of the parish church, which stands above the Meon estuary, has been dated to the late 7th century, which makes it the oldest Christian building in Wessex.

The other major feature of this fascinating church is the Southampton Monument, which stands in a chapel at the east end of the south aisle. This lofty pile includes effigies of the 2nd Earl of Southampton (1545–81), who paid for it, together with those of his mother and his father, who founded the family fortunes and made Place House, formerly Titchfield Abbey, his principal seat. The abbey was founded in 1232 for the White Monks of Premonstré, France, by Peter des Roches, bishop of Winchester. The fine Tudor ruin which can now be seen is all that remains of the later grand house that the 1st Earl of Southampton built on the abbey site in 1538. Nearby is a huge medieval tithe barn.

The 3rd Earl of Southampton (1573–1624) built an iron-mill, above Titchfield at Funtley, which was later to become famous in the hands of the pioneer ironmaster Henry Cort (1740–1800). The 3rd Earl also closed off the estuary of the Meon at Hillhead, which finally extinguished Titchfield's modest pretensions as a port. The logic of this manoeuvre is obscure, but it was probably an attempt to reclaim the marshy lands of Titchfield Haven. These lands now hold one of the most important nature reserves in the area. Another legacy of the scheme is the fine path that runs alongside the small canal, between the east side of the church and the Meon Shore.

The 3rd Earl's greatest claim to fame is that he was Shakespeare's patron. Despite much effort, however, no definite proof of any connection between the poet or his plays and Titchfield has ever been found, though an old plan of Place House shows a 'Play Room'. Was the Bard ever there?

The minor road that runs by Place House provides a pleasant route up the western side of the Meon Valley to the A333, which it meets a mile to the west of **Wickham**. The A32 road from Fareham also passes through Wickham

Henry Cort and Funtley
There were several places where iron-making was carried out in Hampshire, notably in response to the needs of the dockyard at Portsmouth. The most important of these was on the river Meon at Funtley, where the ironmaster and inventor Henry Cort (1740–1800) carried out experiments on the production of wrought iron.

In 1783 and 1784 he was granted patents for processes in which iron was hot-rolled into bars and pig-iron was puddled to produce wrought iron.

Henry Cort lived in Gosport, though his partner, Samuel Jellicoe, lived on site, in Funtley House. Jellicoe died in 1789 owing nearly £40,000 to the Navy Board. Cort was ruined, though he was later granted a pension by parliament. Within a few years of Cort's discoveries Britain's position as an importer of wrought iron had been changed to that of a net exporter.

Place House, Titchfield

and continues further north along the length of the upper Meon Valley. This was the coach route to London via Alton and is the prettiest way to reach north Hampshire from the Solent.

Wickham is probably a medieval planned town, perhaps laid out after rights to a market and fair were granted in 1268. At this time the manor house stood on the opposite side of the A32, south of the present church. Even earlier, Wickham was of some importance as a station on the Roman road that ran between the port at Bitterne, near Southampton, and Chichester.

Wickham's most famous son, William of Wickham, was humbly born as William Long and rose to great office as the bishop of Winchester and founder of Winchester College and New College, Oxford. As far as I know, he is totally uncommemorated in his birthplace.

One of the most attractive roads in the village is Bridge Street, which runs out of the north-east corner of the square and leads to the river and the church. It winds down a steep terrace, past Chesapeake Mill, which dates from 1820 and takes its name from the captured American frigate which provided many of its timbers. The countryside to the north-east of Wickham is heavily wooded and very peaceful. There are several car parks.

The string of villages that make up the Meon Valley between Wickham and East Meon are amongst the prettiest in Hampshire. Until 1955 the valley had its own railway, which linked Fareham with Alton. The old station at **Droxford** has been converted into a delightful private house. Near by is a plaque recording that Churchill and his staff met here in 1944, immediately prior to D-Day.

Corhampton has a remarkably well-preserved Saxon church, which was once a chapel of Titchfield Abbey. The centre of **Exton**, with its famous Shoe Inn, lies off the A32. It is one of the few public places where the river can be enjoyed. There is a very pleasant walk from Exton to Beacon Hill and beyond to the site of the deserted village of Lomer, which was once held by Titchfield church.

Warnford is a funny sort of village: it was once centred in the park, but progressively the villagers were edged out by the lords of the manor so that the church now stands on its own, in open parkland (the mansion house has gone). It is well worth walking from the road along the public footpath to the church and ruined medieval manor house.

West Meon is famous as the burial place of Thomas Lord, the founder of Lord's Cricket Ground. His grave, which lies to the south of the church, was restored in 1955, to commemorate the bicentenary of his birth. The village pub was named in his honour at the same time.

East Meon has a huge church for its size of village. It was built in about 1150 by Henry of Blois, bishop of Winchester, and is sometimes referred to as the 'cathedral of the downs'. It was once at the centre of the East Meon Hundred, a huge estate, which belonged to the bishops of Winchester. The court house of 1397 still stands to the south-east of the church.

Old Winchester Hill, which rises to a height of 648ft, is a rare relic of old Hampshire downland. It stands above Warnford and is managed by the Nature Conservancy. A way-marked path leads from the car parks to the summit of the hill, which is surmounted by a well-preserved Iron Age fort and a few Bronze Age burial mounds. There are superb views all round. A plaque points to the sights.

This is the place to take a quiet stroll through the deep shade of the yew wood (the climax vegetation on chalk), across the flower-rich grasslands (with masses of orchids), in the company of whistling larks and cackling woodpeckers. Most of Hampshire's uplands were once like this, maintained, like the

Gosport

Population: 70,705

Early Closing: Wed

Cashpoints: *Barclays* 43/44 High St; *Lloyds* 20/24 High St, 220 Forton Rd; *Midland* 26 High St; *NatWest* 7 Stokesway, Stokes Rd

Tourist Information: Falkland Gardens (summer only)

Attractions: Royal Navy Submarine Museum and HMS *Alliance*, Fort Brockhurst, Spit Bank Fort*

Leisure: Holbrook Recreation Centre

Cinema: Ritz

By Road: London 82 miles (A32, M27), Fareham 6 miles (A32), Portsmouth 13 miles (A32, A27)

By Rail: The nearest main line station is at Portsmouth (1hr 40mins from London)

reserve, by the constant grazing of sheep. Intensive farming (and intensive eating by city dwellers!) has all but destroyed this type of downland. What happens if the sheep are taken away can be seen in three small fenced-in squares to the north of the hill-fort, in which dense scrub thrives.

This fragment of downland is a nature reserve by accident. It is in parts too steep to be ploughed and during the last war it served as a mortar range. It was taken over by the Nature Conservancy in 1954, who soon found that it was littered with unexploded bombs. Many are still there; the areas which have not been 'swept' are clearly marked and fenced.

GOSPORT

Like most maritime towns, Gosport starts off with a bang at the water's edge and peters out inland. It is an echo of Portsmouth, a service and a Services town that once was preoccupied with storing the biscuits and bully beef of the Royal Navy, ferrying its ammunition and giving solace to its men. Its mother port is a few minutes away by ferry, or half an hour by car.

In the summer a regular boat trip runs to Spit Bank Fort (also reached from Clarence Pier, Southsea, and the Isle of Wight), the Palmerston fort which stands in the sea 2 miles off Blockhouse Point. It is a considerable experience to explore this great mass of granite, 50yds in diameter. It cost £214,000 to build in 1862–78 and has its own artesian water supply. Fort Brockhurst on the northern outskirts of Gosport is also open to the public and contains a fine exhibition on the defences of Portsmouth Harbour.

There are remains of earlier, probably 18th-century, defences to the south of the Gosport ferry terminus, beyond Holy Trinity church. Further south is **Haslar Lake**, a tidal inlet that was once the estuary of the river Alver. It is

crossed by a bridge which leads to the Haslar
district of Gosport, which has long been
dominated by the Navy. Haslar Hospital, the
home of the Institute of Naval Medicine, dates
from the middle of the 18th century and was a
pioneering foundation of its day.

Haslar is also the home of submariners. The
Royal Navy Submarine Museum at HMS
Dolphin tells the story from the earliest days. Its
prime exhibits are three submarines, namely
the huge HMS *Alliance*, a World War II vintage
vessel (though it never went into battle), the
1901 vintage *Holland I* and the fascinating
midget submarine or X-craft. Visitors are first
given a navy-style pre-visit audiovisual
briefing, followed by a tour of the *Alliance* in
the company of former submariners. There is a
large conventional museum. A visit is bound to
leave impressions of an experience beyond the
ken of most of us.

The centre of Gosport's victualling
operations, another of its key naval activities,
was Royal Clarence Yard, to the north of the
ferry. It was here that Queen Victoria alighted
at a special station to board the royal yacht for
Osborne House, her country home on the Isle
of Wight. The railway reached Gosport, via
Southampton, in 1841, long before Portsmouth
acquired its own line in 1859. Gosport's
magnificent, though derelict station at the
north end of Spring Garden Lane was
designed by Sir William Tite.

North of Clarence Yard is **Priddy's Hard**,
the Royal Naval Armaments Depot, where
conventional weapons (and no doubt more
lethal products) were until recently taken out
to the ships in considerable quantities. The
original powder magazine of 1771, when the
site was first developed, now holds the Naval
Ordnance Museum, which tells the story of
naval gunnery, from the round shot of Nelson
to the missiles of the Falklands. There is a fine
collection of torpedoes.

Spit Bank Fort

Combat and duelling
Judicial combat under the law was once a way of setting disputes that would now reach the courts.

Duelling as such did not become common until the 16th century. It grew up in France and reached a peak during the reign of Louis XIV. In England most duels were fought in the 18th century, when such prominent men as Lord Byron, Sheridan, Pitt the Elder and Canning became embroiled in disputes of honour.

The last duel in England, fought at Gosport in 1845, was between Lt C Hawkey of the Royal Marines and a Captain Seton of the 11th Dragoons, who allegedly made advances to Mrs Hawkey against her wishes in the King's Room, Southsea, then a fashionable meeting place. Hawkey offered Seton a public horse-whipping, but he chose the duel, in which he was mortally wounded. The public attitude to duelling at the time is clear from the fact that Hawkey was charged with manslaughter. But after a trial at Winchester, amidst extraordinary nationwide publicity, he was acquitted on grounds of Seton's provocation and the possibility that the dragoon had in fact died as a consequence of surgery needed to remove the bullet.

The story of Gosport is told in its own museum in the High Street. This makes clear that the village of **Alverstoke** was of considerable importance in the early history of Gosport. The area around Alverstoke church still has the feel of a village, though the existing church is almost entirely Victorian. The original church is said to have been built by Henry of Blois, bishop of Winchester (or perhaps by King Stephen) in thanks for deliverance from a storm, which gave the town the name God's Port.

There are some fascinating traces of an ambitious Victorian development to be found south of Alverstoke church. This is the small district of Anglesey, called after the Marquis who in 1826 built the Crescent, a fine curving terrace which still stands. It was the first part of a grand scheme to bring wealthy visitors and residents to this part of Gosport, though it did not immediately live up to expectations. However, in the 1840s a Mr Robert Cruickshank successfully developed the area.

Stokes Bay is Gosport's seaside. It is backed by Stanley Park, a pleasant wooded area of evergreens and shrubs which is open to the public. The breezy shingle coastlands of the bay continue all the way to the edges of Lee-on-Solent, across Browndown, a remote area of military dereliction and waste land. It is no surprise to find that the last recorded formal duel in England was fought here, in 1845.

The main feature of **Lee-on-Solent** is a 2-mile esplanade and shingle beach, backed by Nice-style apartments. It is popular with windsurfers and weekend sailors. An Air Day is held each year at the naval airfield, which also contains the recently commercialised search-and-rescue centre for the whole Solent area.

Between Lee and Gosport is the Wild Grounds nature reserve, which covers some 67 acres of scrubland and woods skirted by the river Alver. Formerly used by the military, it was acquired by Gosport in 1966. It can be visited by permit.

HAVANT

In 1974 the south-east corner of Hampshire, which has grown dramatically since the last war, was for the first time granted borough status. The borough is centred on Havant and includes Emsworth, Hayling Island and the whole of the shoreline from the Sussex border to the edge of Farlington Marshes. It takes in part of the great harbours of Langstone and Chichester and includes the housing estates of Leigh Park and the modern town of Waterlooville – a straggly sort of area invented by local government officers, yet it is almost exactly the same as the ancient Bosmere Hundred, recorded in Domesday Book!

Havant itself is a convenient centre with good shopping and a local museum. The town was for 1,000 years an important centre for fellmongering, ie working with parchment and leather. The centrepiece of the museum is a unique collection of guns made by the engineer Cecil G Vokes, who lived in Hampshire and invented the automatic windscreen wiper and other devices for the motor car. Scalextric toys were first made in Havant in 1956, when their inventor, Fred Francis, set up a factory at Leigh Park.

Apart from the church, the oldest building in the town is the 'Old House at Home' in South Street: the rest of Havant seems to have perished in a fire of 1760. The church contains a brass to Thomas Aylwarde, a 15th-century rector and chaplain and secretary to Bishop William of Wickham. East Street and South Street have some pleasant Georgian frontages, whilst the Pallant (echoes of Chichester) and nearby streets are strollable parts of the old town. Two members of Havant Hockey Club were included in the celebrated English hockey

Havant

Population: 116,649

Early Closing: Wed

Market Days: Tue, Sat

Cashpoints: *Barclays* 18 East St; *Lloyds* 4 West St; *Midland* 48 West St; *NatWest* 2 West St, 23 West St

Tourist Information: 1 Park Rd South

Attraction: Havant Museum and Art Centre

Leisure: Havant Leisure Centre

Arts: Old Town Hall Theatre

By Road: London 70 miles (A3), Portsmouth 9 miles (A27), Southampton 22 miles (A27, M27)

By Rail: 1hr 20mins from London (Waterloo to Portsmouth Harbour line). Direct services to Brighton, Chichester, Petersfield and Portsmouth team that won a gold medal at the 1988 Seoul Olympics.

Emsworth is a fascinating old fishing port and seaside mill town which is well worth exploring. It sits at the head of one arm of Chichester Harbour, on the eastern borders of Hampshire, which here follow the course of the River Ems. The old port of Emsworth, serving Chichester, grew up between two huge estuarine ponds that were impounded to power tide mills.

Between the two mill ponds lay the shipyards of such men as John King and J D Foster, whose names are associated with the remarkable development of the local oyster and scallop business in the late 18th and 19th centuries. Traces of the old oyster ponds can still be seen at low tide.

One of the most pleasant walks in the district runs for 2–3 miles along the top of Chichester Harbour to the Royal Oak at Langstone, one of Hampshire's great pubs. The path starts from the premises of the Emsworth Slipper Sailing Club and curls along the top of the sea-wall that encloses the Seaside Mill Pond. It is an inspiring first leg of two popular long-distance footpaths, namely the 60-mile Solent Way, which leads along the coast to Milford-on-Sea, and the Wayfarer's Walk, a 70-mile jaunt across the county.

Langstone Mill

Although **Langstone** gave its name to the great harbour that lies between Portsmouth and Hayling Island, it is in fact now under the Chichester Harbour Conservancy. It was once the port for Havant and, remarkably, like Portsmouth, came under the Port of Southampton.

Langstone Mill and the Royal Oak were once a 'bread factory' for the Navy and other customers. There were in fact two separate mills together, a tide mill and a windmill. The pub was the bakehouse. The mill was restored in 1932 by the Petersfield artist Flora

Twort. One of her guests was Nevile Norway alias Nevile Shute, who wrote his novel *Pied Piper* there whilst running his own business, Airspeed Aviation, at Portsmouth.

Langstone Harbour is world-famous for the birds which in the winter migrate here from the sub-arctic wastes of Russia. Ornithologists have estimated that three per cent of the world's entire population of dark-bellied Brent geese overwinter in the harbour, whilst another dozen species reach internationally significant numbers. Many of them roost on Farlington Marshes at the head of the harbour. This is managed as a nature reserve and a large part of it is freely open to the public.

Sir George Staunton Country Park is a pleasant surprise in the midst of suburbia on the outskirts of Havant. Ideal for a restful hour or a jaunt with the family, its landscaped gardens were the creation of Sir George Thomas Staunton, who in 1791, as an 11-year-old page-boy, accompanied his father and others on the first British embassy to China. He quickly learned Chinese and made a fortune in the East India Company.

The site is split in two by Middle Park Way. To the south, where the Staunton mansion stood, is an ornamental farm, ideal for children, but noisy. An attractive surviving octagonal library building, designed after a monastic chapter house, now contains an exhibition on Sir George and the estate. It also tells the story of the opening of China to western travellers in the late 18th century. The remains of the home farm of 1821, and other buildings, house a collection of rare breeds of poultry and other animals – a delight for children.

On the north side of the site, landscaped parklands fall down to a grand lake (being restored), complete with a Chinese bridge and several islands. There is also a 'shell-house' and a few other relics of the gardens of the

Langstone Harbour
The shore between Fareham and Chichester is part of the 'drowned' coastline of the Solent. It is a complex jigsaw of islands, mudflats and winding channels. Langstone Harbour lies between the islands of Portsea and Hayling. At its head is the former port of Langstone, which once served Havant. It is a harbour which is now used for a wide variety of sports, including sailing, fishing, water-skiing and skin diving.

The mudflats of Langstone are important feeding grounds for many thousands of birds. It is recognised as an area of international importance for wildlife. Visitors can observe the birds from Farlington Marshes, a reserve of the Hampshire and Isle of Wight Naturalists' Trust. Access to the reserve, which juts out into the harbour for a mile or more, is from the A27. The land was reclaimed in the 18th century.

The main bird visitor to Langstone Harbour is the Brent goose, which comes in large numbers to winter here from Russia and other northern climes. About a dozen bird species are reckoned to have internationally significant populations in the harbour, which supports more than 50 species of breeding birds. This is the place to spot such birds as the black-tailed godwit, widgeon, dunlin and many others. Offshore islands support breeding populations of ringed plover, oystercatcher and redshank.

second mansion house, built in 1863 by William Stone, who was Portsmouth's MP for a short while.

Rowland's Castle is a pleasant village set about a long thin green on the Sussex borders of Hampshire. It was once the haunt of smugglers and ne'er-do-wells who lived on the fringes of the Forest of Bere. It sprang to life after it became a stopping-point on the direct London-Portsmouth railway line, which was opened in 1859.

The northern part of the parish includes the hamlet of **Finchdean**, with its interesting village foundry, and **Idsworth**, which has a charming isolated chapel that stands in the middle of a field. It is reached from the road via a wooden bridge across a winterbourne. Until the coming of the railway, the seat of the local landowners, the Clarke-Jervoises, stood to the south of the chapel, where the remains of a walled garden, dovecote and other outbuildings can be seen from a footpath. Another footpath leads in the opposite direction over the downs to **Chalton**, a delightful village 2 miles away. Its tiny green, surrounded by church, farm and the Red Lion pub (a legend in itself), form a classical village setting. Chalton was once the mother parish of Rowland's Castle, Idsworth, Catherington and Clanfield. The site of a notable Anglo-Saxon settlement has been excavated on the nearby hill, but there is nothing to see on the surface.

HAYLING ISLAND

The different fates of the two great low-lying islands which stand off the south coast of Hampshire could scarcely have been more marked. One became Hayling Island and the other became Portsmouth. It was the need for a bridge (amongst other things) that kept the human tide from Hayling and it was not until 1824 that it became linked to the mainland, largely at the instigation of the lord of the manor, the Duke of Norfolk.

Pedestrians can cross to the island on the Eastney ferry, which plies regularly across the mouth of Langstone Harbour. There is also a footpath which crosses almost the entire length of the island, from the road bridge in the north to Station Road in the south. It runs through almost deserted countryside along the route of the old Hayling Billy Line, which was opened in 1867 and closed in about 1965.

Hayling has a superb weather record and exudes the instant devil-may-care atmosphere of a holiday island. There are several holiday camps (some open to day visitors) and sailing clubs along its eastern coast. It has all the facilities one would expect of a smallish seaside resort, with a funfair and a huge outdoor water chute at the Amusement Park, which is opposite Beach Road. Near by stand Norfolk Crescent and the Royal Hotel, the earliest seaside buildings on Hayling. They date from 1825 (the year after the first bridge) and were intended to make it a posh resort (cf the Crescent at Alverstoke).

The conglomeration of bungalows, beach huts and seaside villas that now cover the island obscure traces of the original rural community that for centuries lived here. Before the bridge was built the farmers and their animals reached the mainland by wading across at low tide. (Beware: the wadeway is now deeper!) Old maps show that salterns were worked on the northern and eastern shores, hence the names Salterns Lane and Salterns Close at Mengham. Pretty thatched cottages and neat farms can still be seen in the north and east of the island, whilst two medieval churches and the old manor house of 1777 survive. The latter has a huge barn, 45 yards in length.

Northney in the north-east of Hayling is a world-famous centre for windsurfing, as befits the island where this popular sport was

John Goodyer (1592–1664)
This distinguished
Petersfield resident was one
of the first botanists to
make proper scientific
observations of plants. His
meticulous descriptions of
individual species, and lists
of species found in
particular places, set a new
standard. His original notes
still exist and are kept in
the archives of Magdalen
College, Oxford.

John Goodyer's
reputation was such that
when the Civil War broke
out he was able to obtain a
'protection order' from
Lord Hopton, the general
in charge of the Royalist
forces in the area that
included Hampshire. The
document conferring this
protection was discovered
under the floorboards of his
house in Petersfield in 1907.

Another Petersfield
resident of distinction was
John Worlidge (d.1698), an
agriculturalist whose
Systema Agriculturae became
a leading textbook of its
day. He invented a
mechanical seed drill and
championed changes in
farming practice, notably
enclosure, water meadows
and the use of turnips as a
winter food for livestock.

invented by 12-year-old Peter Chilvers in 1958.
This part of the Hampshire coast is ideal for
windsurfing: the sea-front offers Force 4 winds
for the experienced board-sailor, whilst the
sheltered eastern shore caters for the tyro. The
highlight each year is the round-the-island
marathon.

PETERSFIELD

Duchess of Portsmouth, Baroness of Petersfield
and Countess of Fareham was how Charles II
styled Mademoiselle de Querouaille, one of his
mistresses. Why he honoured her in this way
is obscure, but he certainly knew Petersfield
and visited the town several times.

In the heyday of coaching, Petersfield was
an attractive stop on the Portsmouth road (now
the A3). It still is a charming town, though the
best bits are now off the main road. The centre
of the town is to the west, whilst to the east is
its fine heath and lake.

Since Petersfield was founded in the
mid-12th century, the High Street has been its
main street. This runs at right angles to the A3
and leads to the spacious Market Square, one
of the finest in Hampshire. At the centre is a
splendid lead statue, of William III, seated in
classical garb astride a horse. Regular markets
are still held in the square, but they no longer
involve animals, once the mainstay of the
town's income. Sheep Street is the name of a
pretty lane that leads from the square to the
Spain, a sort of 'sub-square'. On the west side
of the Spain is a plaque commemorating John
Goodyer (1592–1664), a famous botanist.

The very satisfying composition of
Petersfield's square is partly due to the fact that
it is overlooked by its parish church. This was
planned in about 1120 as a cruciform church,
with a grand tower at the crossing, but it was
never completed. Amongst the memorials in
the church are several to members of the
Jolliffe family, who were notorious lords of the

manor in the 18th and 19th centuries. In the north-west corner of the churchyard is the tombstone of John Small, who died in 1826 aged 89. He was a local shoemaker who played for the famous Hambledon Cricket Club. He used his craft to make balls.

Lovers of that archetypal 'country town' artist Flora Twort (1893-1986) will soon be able to see some of her work hung in the house where she lived in Church Walk, to the west of the church. Her pictures of the square and of Petersfield's 'Taro' horsefair are classics.

Petersfield High Street offers a delightful mélange of architectural styles. My favourite is 4, the lofty Italianate building now used by the NatWest Bank, which faces the former Corn Exchange at the north-east of the square.

An important piece in the Petersfield jigsaw is Folly Lane, a small thoroughfare that leads from the north side of High Street to College Street. It emerges alongside the Folly Antiques Market, opposite the Red Lion, which is the sole relic of the town's coaching inns. The lane was once the route of the London road (the southern part has been built over) until the remarkably early Portsmouth and Sheet Turnpike of 1711 moved the through route to the present position of the A3.

To the east is Petersfield Heath, 90 acres of common with a large lake in the middle, created in 1741, all of which was fortunately bought by the town in 1913. An annual fair (successor to the horse fair) is held in October and at other times there are pleasant walks, golf, cricket, fishing and boats for hire. In Heath Road, to the north, is the 1930s town hall and a heated open-air swimming pool. The town's leisure centre is at Penns Place.

Petersfield is one of those places whose 'mother parish' is now much less important than her 'daughter'. Until 1886 Petersfield church was under **Buriton**, which can be reached from the Heath via a minor road (or

Petersfield

Population: 10.078

Early Closing: Thu

Market Days: Wed, Sat

Cashpoints: *Barclays* 10 The Square; *Lloyds* 5 The Square; *Midland* Market Square; *NatWest* 4 High St

Tourist Information: The Library, 27 The Square

Attractions: Bear Museum and Dolls' Hospital

Arts: Petersfield Festival Hall

Leisure: The Heath, Petersfield Leisure Centre, Petersfield Outdoor Swimming Pool

By Road: London 59 miles (A3), Winchester 19 miles (A272)

By Rail: 1hr 10mins from London (Waterloo to Portsmouth Harbour line). Direct services to Guildford, Havant and Portsmouth. Connections to Chichester via Havant.

off the A3). It is a picture-book village with a duck pond beside an ironstone 12th-century church. This contains fine monuments to Thomas Bilson (1656–95), one of Petersfield's MPs, and to Thomas Hanbury, who was the first to wrest municipal rights from the people of Petersfield, following his purchase of the borough in 1597. Buriton was often in the thick of local politics, particularly in the 18th century, when the lords of the manor, Edward Gibbon (father, son and grandson), fought the Jolliffes and lost. Edward Gibbon III (1737–94), who lived as a boy in Buriton, was the author of the *Decline and Fall of the Roman Empire*.

The parish of Buriton includes much of Butser Hill and Queen Elizabeth Forest. More than 1,000 acres of dramatic chalk downlands are contained in the Queen Elizabeth Country Park. Its extensive menu of events, including the novel sport of grass-skiing, is masterminded from a modern visitors' centre on the east side of the A3. Opposite is the Butser Ancient Farm, an exciting re-creation of an Iron Age agricultural settlement (about 400 BC) that has an international reputation. One of the sites used by archaeologists is open to the public. It is centred about a great round-house whose clever structure has no central support. It is based on that of a similar one excavated at Pimperne, near Blandford. A herb garden based on the writings of Virgil and Columella contains more than 150 varieties of plants.

The area to the north of Petersfield is also full of drama. This is the hanger country of Hampshire, one of the finest areas of unspoilt countryside in southern England. It takes its name from the steep beech-hung hills that are common hereabouts. Between Petersfield and Alton there are about 100 hangers, each of them formed where the soft greensand meets the harder chalk. They give the area a quite unique character. It is an unspoilt relict landscape, a left-over of the retreat of the last

William III, Petersfield

Ice Age. Several near-extinct species of *Red Data Book* insects are found here. Narrow roads, worn deep by countless cartwheels, wind from hamlet to hamlet, beneath beech woods, with occasional breathtaking views of the countryside below. The Hangers Way is a 20-mile path between Petersfield and East Worldham. The leg to Hawkley is especially dramatic.

The best-known hanger is probably **Stoner Hill**, which winds up out of Petersfield from Bell Hill, a turning off the A272 at a round-about to the west of the town. Halfway up the hanger is a turning to the right to Steep, home of Bedales School, a famous public school that pioneered new approaches to education in the 1890s. It was founded by J H Badley in Sussex and moved to Hampshire in 1900.

At the top of Stoner Hill is a turning to the right into Cockshott Lane, **Froxfield**, where the poet Edward Thomas (1878–1917) once lived and where can be found the workshops and showroom of Edward Barnsley (1900-87), a craftsman whose furniture is amongst the delights of the 20th century. His son now runs the business. Edward Thomas discovered his metier as poet relatively late and was killed during World War I. A regular walk takes place on his birthday, 3 March, organised by the Edward Thomas Fellowship. It covers the countryside he loved, including the Shoulder of Mutton Hill, where since 1937 there has stood a memorial to him.

Almost anywhere in the hanger country is a delight. There is a pleasant ride (in fact, several different rides) from Petersfield to Hawkley Hanger, part of which in 1774 subsided after heavy rains. The landslip left a cliff 69ft high and 750ft long, as recorded by Gilbert White in his *Natural History* (Letter XLV). The cottage now called 'Slip Cottage' and a pond were cataclysmically moved. Hawkley church is an intriguing neo-Norman building of 1865.

Edward Thomas (1878–1917)
South London was Edward Thomas's stamping ground, though both his parents were of Welsh stock. His father worked as a staff clerk at the Board of Trade and was a practising Unitarian. Thomas was encouraged to write whilst still at school by James Noble, a sometime editor of the *Liverpool Argus*. He fell in love with one of Noble's daughters, Helen, who became pregnant whilst he was still at Oxford. The couple married and, after graduating in 1900, Thomas lived the life of the writer. He earned his living as a book reviewer and from commissioned titles such as *Beautiful Wales*, *The Heart of England* and *The South Country*. Between 1906 and going to war in 1916 he lived with his family in three successive houses at Steep and Froxfield, near Petersfield.

Literary critics now say that Thomas's efforts at prose were 'tedious' and the 'wrong medium for what he wanted to express'. When World War I broke out there were no longer any commissions for the writer and so he wrote for himself. The result was the outpouring of poetry. His best-known poem is probably *Adelstrop*, but the one with the most intriguing local links is his very first poem, *Up in the Wind*, which was written in December 1914. It is set in the White Horse Inn, Prior's Dean, distinguished by having a signpost with an empty frame.

A few miles north of Hawkley is **Selborne**, one of the most-visited villages in Hampshire. People come to visit Gilbert White's house, and to see his grave and the stained-glass memorial window in the church. This famous clergyman, who never rose beyond the humble position of curate, wrote one of the bestsellers of all time, *The Natural History of Selborne*, first published in 1789. There are delightful walks across the common he knew and up the zig-zag path he and his brother cut. The house he lived in, 'The Wakes', once his grandfather's home, now holds the Gilbert White Museum. It was purchased in 1954 after a generous donation from bibliophile Robert Oates (1874–1958) and also contains material devoted to two of Oates' famous forebears, both explorers. These are Frank Oates (1840–75) and Captain Lawrence Oates (1880–1912), whose famous last words were: 'I'm just going outside. I may be some time.'

Caravans are restored and decorated in traditional style at Limes End Yard, Selborne, where there is also the only Romany Museum in England to be run by gypsy people. According to its founder, Peter Ingram, only a dozen bands of true gypsies remain in the whole of Britain.

For 24 years Gilbert White was curate of the neighbouring village of **Farringdon** (Upper Farringdon on the map), journeying each Sunday from Selborne to take services. Another interesting man to serve the village was T H Massey, who was rector from 1857 to 1919. He built the chancel and vestry of the church, also the rectory, and then put his energies into 'Massey's Folly', a huge red-brick-and-tile monstrosity built with the aid of three workmen. It still stands.

Beyond the hangers the countryside of east Hampshire changes drastically. To the east are the flat sandy commons that seem irresistible to military authorities. Bordon and Longmoor

Massey's Folly, Farringdon

Camps are etched in the minds of many a soldier, whilst the commons of Kingsley and Shortheath and Woolmer Forest are all subject to the byelaws of Aldershot Military Lands.

Fortunately, large areas of this part of Hampshire were amongst the first acquisitions of the National Trust, namely Ludshott Common and Bramshott Chase in 1908, and Waggoner's Wells in 1919. The series of delightful ponds beneath the beech woods of **Waggoner's Wells** were probably hammer ponds used for iron-making. They feed one arm of the River Wey, which leads via Bramshott, Passfield Common (another National Trust property) and Headley to meet the Alton arm of the river at Tilford. Behind **Bramshott** church is a large military cemetery containing the graves of 330 Canadians who were stationed in the area during World War I. **Headley** has the only wholly water-powered mill still worked in Hampshire. It is a reminder that this stretch of the River Wey was once as important, industrially, as any modern corporate park.

Bramshott is the mother parish of **Liphook**, which, like Petersfield, grew to cater for the needs of travellers on the Portsmouth road. No fewer than six roads meet in the centre of Liphook. Just to the south of the junction is the Royal Anchor Inn, a famous hostelry where Queen Victoria, Lord Nelson and many others stayed. Further south is Liphook Post Office, which is graced by the bust of Flora Thompson (1876–1947), author of *Lark Rise to Candleford*, who lived and worked here from 1916 to 1927. Further south again is Bohunt Manor, whose gardens and lake are open to the public in aid of the World Wildlife Fund. To the east of Liphook is the Hollycombe Steam Collection, an enthusiast's paradise. One ticket will let you listen to a steam organ, ride on a steam roundabout, take a trip on a tiny quarry steam train, have a quiet 'steam' picnic and more.

Bramshott and the Canadians

The row upon row of military graves in the lower churchyard at Bramshott are there because Bramshott Common was once a vast encampment for Canadian troops. It became known as 'Tin Town' and 'Mudsplosh Camp' and was first used during World War I. Many of the graves contain the remains of men who died in the savage influenza epidemic of 1918.

Canadians were also stationed at Bramshott during the last war, when they took over a 600-bed hospital, but the main base for the Canadian Army in Britain at that time was at Aldershot. Camps built in Bramshott during 1939–45 were called after the Great Lakes – Huron, Ontario and Erie. All traces of the camps have now gone, and the open spaces of the common have been regained, though the church still contains many reminders of these days. The east window shows the names and coats-of-arms of the states of Canada, whilst the nave contains commemorative furnishings and flags. Each year the sacrifices made by these men are remembered at a thanksgiving service held in the church.

Bramshott is an example of a parish in which the original settlement, around the church, has been dramatically overtaken by developments elsewhere in the parish, in this case at Liphook, which has blossomed alongside the A3.

Southampton

Population: 214,802

Market Days: Thu, Fri, Sat

Cashpoints: *Barclays* 5/6 Manchester St, 70 University Rd, 30 High St, 425/7 Shirley Rd; *Lloyds* 125 Above Bar, 77 Shirley High St, 413 Bitterne Rd Bitterne, 1 Victoria Rd Woolston; *Midland* 165 High St, 390A Bitterne Rd, 14 The Broadway Portswood, 24 London Rd, 403 Shirley Rd, Southampton General Hospital Tremona Rd; *NatWest* 1 Romsey Rd Shirley, 1 Manor Farm Rd Bitterne, 12 High St, 194 Above Bar, 405 Romsey Rd Maybush, 2 Portsmouth Rd Woolston.

Tourist Information: Above Bar Shopping Precinct, M27 Rownhams Services

Attractions: Bargate Guildhall Museum, God's House Tower, Hall of Aviation, Southampton Maritime Museum, Tudor House Museum

Arts: Art Gallery, Gantry Theatre, The Guildhall, Mayflower Theatre, Mountbatten Theatre, Nuffield Theatre, Turner Sims Concert Hall

Leisure: Bitterne Bowl, Bitterne Pool, Bitterne Leisure Centre, Centre 2000, Municipal Golf Course, Oaklands Leisure Centre, Oaklands Pool, St Mary's Leisure Centre, Southampton Sports Centre

Cinemas: Cannon, Mountbatten, Odeon

3 Southampton and the Solent

This is the part of Hampshire dominated by yachting. It is a business that has boomed since the war and shows no sign of stopping. The Southampton International Boat Show has become a very important event on the yachting calendar. The marinas of the Hamble River and Southampton Water contain more boats than any other part of Britain. Here exists a very special concentration of skills that reflect a long tradition of designing and making boats.

For centuries, boats built on the Solent were for merchants. Then came the Royal Navy. Admiralty ships were initially constructed at Southampton, and later at Bursledon, Buckler's Hard and elsewhere, though the permanent RN Dockyard came to be situated at Portsmouth. The Vosper Thornycroft yard at Woolston, near Southampton, still makes special types of ships for naval use. When the aircraft industry 'took off' during World War I, shipwrights' skills were applied to seaplanes and other craft. It was a trend which ultimately led to the Spitfire, designed and made in Hampshire, which played a major part in the success of the Battle of Britain. Parts for jet aircraft are still made in the area, at Hamble.

Since Victorian times Southampton has thrived as a port, first out of the docks at the eastern approaches to the River Itchen, then further west, beside a quay 1½ miles long, and most recently from the container port at Millbrook. During the golden age of luxury liners, it was at Southampton that Hollywood stars and the world's rich caught their first glimpse of England, from the decks of such great ships as the *Queen Mary* and *Queen Elizabeth*. The QE2 occasionally still docks at Southampton, but the main focus of interest in the city has moved back to the wharves of the

Itchen and the basins of the Eastern Docks, which are being redeveloped as marinas.

The first such development was at Shamrock Quay, Northam, which has become a pleasant venue for a drink and a meal. It is also a place where the serious yachtsman can find almost anything he needs. Most of the new development however, is in the Eastern Docks, where Ocean Village and the luxurious premises of the Royal Southampton Yacht Club offer a ritzier atmosphere.

Southampton is a strong cultural centre, with two major theatres, several museums, a celebrated art gallery, a large university and the studios of both the BBC and TVS. It is also the home of the Ordnance Survey, the Ford Transit van, Pirelli General and the Esso oil refinery, Fawley. The Southampton Geothermal Heating Company is a unique enterprise that pipes hot water from the depths of the earth to city centre offices.

The fortunes of this part of Hampshire have come from a unique combination of gentle shores and extended high tides. Almost every inlet and harbour on the Solent and Southampton Water is involved in some way with the yachting business. Some parts have been totally overwhelmed by the marina. In others, the more traditional character of the Hampshire coast survives – at places like Netley, Ashlett and Eling. The western shore of Southampton Water, which is called the Waterside, has seen a great deal of development, but it is still pleasantly remote.

Amongst the highlights are the historic dockside and the museums of Southampton, particularly the Hall of Aviation. Well worth a visit outside the city are the Hampshire Farm Museum at Botley, Eling Tide Mill, Calshot Castle and Exbury Gardens. The Lower Test Nature Reserve at Totton and Southampton Common offer contrasting versions of 'peace and quiet'.

By Road: London 76 miles (A33, M3), Winchester 13 miles (A33)

By Rail: 1hr 20mins from London (Waterloo to Weymouth line). Direct services to Bournemouth, Eastleigh, Portsmouth, Romsey and Salisbury. Connections to Havant via Portsmouth and Lymington via Brockenhurst

Southampton International Boat Show

Once you have been to the Boat Show at Southampton the idea of holding such an event in the centre of London seems absurd. Where better to pick a boat than at Southampton, where a specially constructed marina allows complete novices to try out a variety of designs in safety, and with top-class advice on hand.

The show, which is held in September under the auspices of the British Marine Industries Federation, is unashamedly a window display aimed at easing money from the pockets of visitors. Yet it provides an unrivalled opportunity to compare one product with another and catch up with the latest in everything to do with boating, from 'rope to radar' as the promoters say. Also, it makes a great day out for the landlubber who has no intention of ever venturing on the briny. The atmosphere is as relaxed as that of a country show, with boats instead of cows!

The Boat Show is centred on Mayflower Park, alongside the Royal Pier. It was first held in 1969, when 35 exhibitors tentatively displayed their wares on Southampton's dockside. It has now gained an international reputation and is *the* place to plan next year's sailing.

SOUTHAMPTON

Most visitors to Southampton leave without seeing its best bits. This is because the main shopping centre in Above Bar is quite separate from the waterfront and other areas. To solve the problem, the city is planning an elevated 'people mover' railway, which should help to connect the various parts of the city.

The city's main delights are, to the south, the old town and its medieval walls, Ocean Village, the central baths, the historic waterfront and a clutch of museums (mainly free). To the north are 2,000 acres of parkland and commons, the art gallery and also a 2,250-seat theatre with national shows, including opera and ballet. On the outskirts is the university campus, with its theatre, concert hall and gallery, and the sports centre, which has dry ski slopes. Each September the city holds the justly famous Southampton International Boat Show.

Any visit to the city should start at the waterfront. A convenient base, with free parking, is Ocean Village, an exciting new residential 450-berth marina built around the original dock basin of 1842. Although the full facilities of Ocean Village are available only to those who have a mooring and a waterside house, it is a truly public facility and the casual visitor will find plenty to do. The centrepiece is Canute's Pavilion (King Canute is said to have 'stopped the tide' at Southampton), with eating places and shops selling mainly leisure goods. The maritime story of Southampton can be soaked up in a small cinema on the dockside, whilst the maritime museum (presently in the Wool House) will soon become part of the Maritime Heritage Centre at Ocean Village. In the summer, cruises leave here for Southampton Water, the Isle of Wight and the Hamble River. Cruises on board the *Waverley*, 'the last sea-going paddle steamer in the world', leave from the western docks.

Just to the north of Ocean Village, near the Itchen Bridge, is the Southampton Hall of Aviation, which was inspired by the Spitfire saga. This famous aircraft was created at the Supermarine Works on the Woolston side of the river. It evolved from aircraft built for the Schneider Trophy, which the company won outright in 1931 with the Supermarine 6B aircraft. A similar machine is on display in the museum, together with a Spitfire and other aircraft with local connections. The entire museum is built around a huge Sandringham flying-boat. Visitors can clamber aboard and daydream about the days when Imperial Airways (later BOAC) operated services from Southampton to all parts of the British Empire.

Half a mile to the west is God's House Tower, a defence work which takes its name from the medieval hospital that once stood nearby. The tower now houses the city's Museum of Archaeology, including a large display on the Saxon town of Hamwic, or Hamtun (about AD721–840). This lay to the north-east, in the St Mary's district of the city, and was one of the largest towns of its time. It probably gave its name to the medieval town that grew up to the south-west and became South-Hampton. God's House Tower contains fascinating finds from the medieval town and also from the Roman settlement in the area, which was on the east bank of the river at Bitterne (cf Portchester Castle).

Just to the west of the museum is the original church of God's House, which since the time of Elizabeth I has been used as a place of worship by French Protestants. An annual service in French is still held. The heart of the medieval waterfront lay further west, at the foot of High Street, which led to Town Quay. The remains of the water-gate still stand at the east end of Porters Lane. Nearby are the ruins of six medieval houses, notably 'Canute's Palace', and upper-hall house of about 1150.

R J Mitchell (1895–1937)
In his role as Chief Designer for the Supermarine Aviation Works at Woolston, Reginald Mitchell designed the Spitfire, an aircraft which played a crucial role in the Battle of Britain. The prototype first took off from Eastleigh (now Southampton Airport) in March 1936. Although Mitchell lived to see the Ministry of Defence place quantity orders for his machine, by June 1937 he had succumbed to a fatal illness. Eventually, more than 22,500 Spitfires were to be built, many of them financed by special Spitfire Funds set up throughout the country.

'R J', as he was known, was born in Stoke-on-Trent and whilst still at school became fascinated by the inventions then being made in the USA by the Wright Brothers. He trained to be a mechanic with a firm of locomotive engineers and later moved into the drawing office. In 1917 at the age of 22 he obtained a job as personal assistant to Hubert Scott-Paine, the Southampton entrepreneur, who had just become the owner of Supermarine. 'R J' subsequently developed his engineering skills to the full on a series of aircraft designed for the Schneider Races. In addition to the Spitfire, he designed 23 other types of aircraft, including such stalwarts as the Seal, Seagull and Southampton. For ever innovative, R J Mitchell was a prime example of the right man at the right time.

The Pilgrim Fathers
The group of strict puritans who left Southampton for the New World in 1620 have been regarded as the founders of the United States. In fact, there were several earlier attempts to settle the new lands, including the first to succeed, which set out in 1607 to found the Colony of Virginia. Only 10 years before 'The Lost Colony' had left Portsmouth on an ill-fated mission instigated by Sir Walter Raleigh.

The Pilgrim Fathers were religious refugees from Lincolnshire who had first attempted to settle in Holland. At Southampton they were joined by a young cooper from the town, John Alden, and set sail in two boats, the *Mayflower* and the *Speedwell*. The first leg of the journey was fraught with difficulties, as the *Speedwell*, which had been built at Southampton, proved unseaworthy. The puritans therefore put in at Dartmouth and then at Plymouth before setting out in the *Mayflower* by itself. When they landed on what are now the shores of Massachusetts, they named their settlement Plymouth.

The Mayflower Monument was unveiled in Southampton in 1913. It has become the totem pole of Anglo-American friendship and contains a variety of plaques, including one which records the fact that 2 million American troops left Southampton on and after D-Day, 6 June 1944.

It should be compared with the splendid 13th-century merchant's house at 58 French Street, which has been beautifully restored and is managed by English Heritage. At the west end of Porters Lane is a fine brick warehouse of 1860, now used by Geddes Restaurant, which is called after the 'surveyor' whose name is recorded on its west gable.

This is the part of the waterfront from which local ferries leave. There is a frequent service from the east side of Town Quay, across Southampton Water to Hythe. Ferry and hydrofoil services to Cowes on the Isle of Wight leave to the west of the quay, alongside the Royal Pier. With the exception of the 'Brighton Pavilion' pierhead, which contains a restaurant, the pier is due for demolition, following a serious fire. On the opposite side of the road are the Wool House, built by the monks of Beaulieu Abbey in the 14th century, and the dazzlingly white yacht club of 1846, which served for many years as the clubhouse of the Royal Southern Yacht Club (now at Hamble). The Wool House contains the city's fine maritime museum, but its collections will shortly be redisplayed at Ocean Village.

West of the pier is Mayflower Park, a pleasant place to sit and stare (except when occupied by the Boat Show!). It takes its name from the Mayflower Monument opposite, which commemorates the fact that the Pilgrim Fathers left from Southampton in 1620. Beside the monument is the start of a planned 'wall walk' which will provide visitors with a traffic-free path to the city centre. The route will follow the line of the medieval wall, most of which still stands on this side of the town. What follows is an alternative to the 'wall walk'.

The first length of the old wall leads to the Medieval Merchants Hall (about 1410), first recognised as such in 1973. Alongside is the West Gate, where Henry V and his troops embarked for Agincourt. Hereabouts, in the second half of the 18th century, the Walter Taylor family (father, son and grandson) devised the first machine tools, for making wooden pulley blocks for sailing ships. To the west of the old walls, on land that was once under water, can be seen the colourful flumes of Centre 2000, Southampton's zany swimming baths and leisure centre. This part of the city is topped by the spire of St Michael's church, which was built by the Normans shortly after the Conquest. The tower (*sans* spire) was part of the original structure. The church contains the tomb of Sir Richard Lyster, Lord Chief Justice of England from 1546 to 1552, who lived in the Tudor House to the west. This fine timbered building, which is in fact considerably older than its name suggests, now houses one of the city's museums. Its collection covers domestic items of mainly Victorian vintage. It also holds a fine collection of dolls and dolls' houses. A garden at the rear has been laid out in the Tudor style, complete with bee skep, secret garden and heraldic decorations. At the foot of the garden is an arch from St Denys Priory, which gave its name to a northern suburb of the city. A tunnel at the foot of the garden leads to one of the city's treasures, a ruined Norman house. Prior to land reclamation carried on between the wars, its gun-ports (the earliest known in Britain) faced the curving strand of Southampton's western shore, which lay beside the walls.

Tudor House Museum

Further north is Castle Square, where Jane Austen lived briefly (1807–9), though the site of her house is not known. An archway leads from the 'square' through the arcaded north wall of the bailey of the Norman castle, whose keep stood to the south. The castle watergate can be seen below Cement Terrace. Beyond the bailey wall are fine stretches of the old city walls, including two towers and the first bridge of the planned 'wall walk'.

The Blitz
Both Southampton and
Portsmouth suffered
terribly during the last war.
In Portsmouth, more than
6,000 premises were totally
destroyed, including the
Guildhall, the Garrison
Church, eight schools, a
hospital, four cinemas and
a music-hall. A total of 930
civilians were killed in the
town and thousands were
injured. Bomb-sites were a
commonplace sight in
Portsmouth for many years.
There were 67 separate
attacks made on the town
by the Luftwaffe, the first
major one on 24 August
1940, followed by a period
of sustained bombing
between 10 January and 10
March in the following
year.

Similar statistics can be
found for Southampton,
which suffered particularly
badly in raids that took
place in November 1940.
More than 600 people were
killed and more than 900
homes were destroyed. In
1940 the heart of the city
was destroyed, together
with several factories,
including Pirelli's, Rank's
flour mills, the Ordnance
Survey and Gabriel Wade's
timber yard.

Numerous books and
articles have described the
chaos, the fear, the tragedy
– and the comradeship – of
the blitz years. One who
lived through it and later
wrote a story about it was
the novelist Nevil Shute,
who had founded Airspeed
Ltd at Portsmouth, and
later published *What
Happened to the Corbetts*.

Castle Lane leads east to the High Street,
which is topped by the Bargate. This familiar
landmark was the main entrance to the old
town from the north. Its machiolated north
front is decorated with the shields of local
families, including the Marquises of Winchester
(three swords) and the Flemings of North
Stoneham (three owls). A granite roundel in
the pavement just to the north of the archway
records the gruesome statistics of the blitz,
which gutted Southampton in the last war.

In the 18th and 19th centuries, when
Southampton was a sought-after spa town, a
frequent coach service for London left from the
High Street. The Star and the Dolphin are
splendid examples of coaching inns of the
period. A plaque on the Star reveals that the
main road to London was via Alresford and
Alton and the journey took 10 hours. To the
south are the ruins of Holy Rood church,
which was badly hit during the terrible raids of
1940. It now commemorates merchant seamen
and contains memorials to the men of the
Titanic and those lost in the Falklands War.

Southampton's 'High Street' shops are
above the Bargate, in Above Bar Street, which
leads past the Civic Centre, a pioneering (and
very pleasing) complex built before the last
war. It can also be reached from the Bargate via
parkland by turning east into Hanover
Buildings, then north across Houndwell Park,
and north-west across Palmerston Park,
passing *en route* the statue of the great Prime
Minister.

On the north side of the Civic Centre is the
entrance to Southampton Art Gallery, which
has the finest collections of paintings and
sculpture in the south. It subscribes to a wide
spread of styles and periods, but is particularly
strong on 20th-century British art. It also has a
good collection of local scenes. The Baring
Room contains 10 gouache studies of the
Perseus Story by Burne-Jones. Its fine panelling

once adorned the premises of Baring Brothers Bank in the City of London.

North of the Art Gallery is West Park, also called Watts Park after the Southampton hymn-writer Isaac Watts (1674–1748), whose statue stands at the centre. He wrote 'O God, our help in ages past', which peals four times daily from the Civic Centre's clock tower. To the east is the Titanic Memorial, the finest of six local monuments that mourn the ill-fated liner that left Southampton in 1912. This one honours the engineer officers 'who showed their high conception of duty and their heroism by remaining at their posts' as the ship went down.

North of Watts Park is the Bedford Place area of the city, which is a favoured 'village'. Bedford Place itself (actually a street) has a large variety of eating places and some tempting speciality shops, like 'W J French, Bootmakers', who stock expensive shoes. It also contains the offices of *Hampshire; the County Magazine*. Further north are the elegant Regency façades of Carlton Crescent and Rockstone Place. General Gordon of Khartoum fame lived with his sister at 5 Rockstone Place, as recorded on a plaque. There is a memorial to him in Queens Park, to the west of Ocean Village.

Further north are the grounds of Southampton Football Club (The Dell) and the Hampshire County Cricket Club. Here also is the great expanse of Southampton Common, which covers 365 acres (one for every day!) and is the venue for special events. It has an excellent new Studies Centre. East of the common is the popular suburb of Highfield, where Southampton University has been since 1914 (though with full university status only since 1952). Parts of it are open to the public, notably the Nuffield Theatre, which has a repertory company, the Turner Sims Concert Hall and the John Hansard Gallery.

The sinking of the *Titanic*
One of the casualties of the Southampton blitz in 1940 was a plaque in the Central Library which had been put there in 1913 by the local branch of the Amalgamated Musicians Union to commemorate the 'heroic musicians' who continued to play as the *Titanic* went down. The plaque was one of a total of seven that had been erected.

When the *Titanic* left the White Star Dock (later renamed the Ocean Dock) on 10 April 1912 she was regarded as unsinkable. She was one of a trio of superliners designed by the White Star Line as the ultimate in luxury, each of which suffered some bad luck. The *Olympic* had struck a British warship in the previous year, whilst the *Britannic* was sunk by a mine in 1916.

The major scandal of the *Titanic* was not that it had struck an iceberg and sunk but that it had so few lifeboats. If there can ever be any good in the loss of 1,500 lives, it was that thereafter ships were provided with more and better lifeboats.

In 1985 the wreck of the *Titanic* was discovered with the aid of submersibles.

Titantic memorial

North of the common is the city's 300-acre sports centre, a huge complex with all-weather surfaces and facilities for everything from cycle racing to petanque. It helped to make Southampton's reputation as a city which has unrivalled opportunities for leisure. Since the war this reputation has grown, mainly as a result of the yachting boom.

There is scarcely a place on the Hampshire coast that does not have its sailing club and slipway. The main problem for any budding yachtie in recent years has been to find somewhere to moor his boat. The development of marinas, and now residential marinas, may have eased this problem for a few, but there is a continuous pressure for more and more boat spaces. Some say that there are too many boats in the Solent for comfort, others that there is room for more. Whatever the virtues of these arguments, the winsome delights of nosing up deserted creeks and tying up at the pub are gone for ever. Sailing is big business and the Solent is one of its major 'industrial parks'. At the heart of it all are Cowes and the Medina River on the Isle of Wight, and the Hamble River.

Most people first see the Hamble from a car travelling between Southampton and Fareham,

Ocean Village

on the M27 or the A27. From the motorway the view is of motorboats and mud, backed by the black girders of the Bursledon-Fareham railway bridge. From the A27 the scene is one of massed masts and rigging. It is the low height of the road bridge that neatly divides the river into yachts and not-yachts. The great mass of fibreglass and sailcloth immediately below the bridge is mostly within the confines of the boatyard and marina of A H Moody & Sons, a local company which has grown with great skill on the yachting boom. Once content to fulfil contracts to paint the wooden bridge that spanned the river (until 1934), it now has an international reputation and builds yachts for some of the most discerning sailors (and the richest). Each September it hosts the Used Boat Show, an adjunct to the main show in Southampton.

Viewers of the TV soap opera, *Howards' Way*, will instantly recognise the views from the road bridge, for it is here that many of the location shots for the series are filmed. On the **Bursledon** side is the Elephant Boatyard which gets transformed into the 'Mermaid Yard', and facing the bridge across the river is the Jolly Sailor pub, which also frequently features in the story. Closer inspection of the Bursledon area to find 'the Howards' house' and 'the church where Lynne Howard married Claude Dupont' requires some intricate map-reading. Devotees will no doubt have already toured the scene and met some of the cast on one of the *Howards' Way* holidays offered by Southampton City Council and BBC Enterprises Ltd. Bursledon village is reached by turning south off the A27, though the route is tortuous, as the short stretch of road between the railway station car park and the cliff above the Jolly Sailor pub is one-way.

The media fame of Bursledon may be relatively recent, but it was already important in the late Middle Ages, when Admiralty

'Wooden walls'

Naval demands for ships were often so great that contracts were placed with civilian shipbuilders. These were generally for relatively small ships, but even quite large vessels were also built. The ships were generally completed as far as the hull and the fitting was done inside the dockyard. The proximity of Portsmouth, and the availability of timber in the New Forest and elsewhere, meant that contractors in Hampshire were often hired by the Navy Board. The specification and supervision of the work was extremely tight and there were strict penalties for default.

Although some sites, such as those at Bursledon and Buckler's Hard, became permanent shipyards, vessels could be built at any convenient place where launching was possible. Experienced shipwrights became master builders and managed a workforce that might include both local men and gangs from the London yards or the West Country.

To take just one example, in 1691 William Wyatt of Bursledon received a contract from the Navy Board to build the *Devonshire*, a third-rate of 1158 tons. The price agreed was £11 2s 6d per ton. Working to plans drawn up by the Board. Wyatt completed the job within a year, but he lost £1 per ton in the price because the keel was damaged in launching, and there were other defects.

ships built at Southampton were moored and victualled on the Hamble. In the mud above the road bridge lie the remains of the *Grace Dieu*, built for Henry V and the largest vessel of her day – as long as HMS *Victory*. She was struck by lightning and destroyed in 1439. Between 1690 and the early 1800s many large naval ships were built at Bursledon. A tablet on the south wall of St Leonard's church ('where Lynne married Claude') commemorates the greatest of the Hamble shipbuilders, George Parsons, whose yard ('the Mermaid Yard') became called after HMS *Elephant*, Nelson's flagship at the battle of Copenhagen. This was launched at Bursledon in 1786. Another local shipbuilder commemorated in the church is Philemon Ewer, whose tablet in the south transept sweetly calls him an 'ingenious Artist, an excellent Workman and an honest man'.

Other sights to be sought out by intrepid map-readers are the Fox and Hounds pub at Hungerford Bottom (map ref SU 481095) and the 'Howards' house' nearby, in Kew Lane (map ref SU 482094).

One maddening feature of the Hamble River (though one that has preserved much of its charm) is that there is no right of way along its west bank. To travel from Bursledon to **Hamble** village involves a 4-mile detour. For those with a boat, Hamble is a place of almost mystical significance. For the boatless, there are hours of happy sitting and staring. There is a convenient car park on the hard and downstream is the Hamble River Sailing Club, whose members are often picked for the British Olympics team. At race times, binoculars and local know-how are essential to make sense of the manoeuvres of the boats and the apparently meaningless antics in the 'starting box' alongside the clubhouse. Celebrity watchers should concentrate on the Royal Southern Yacht Club, whose cottagey premises and dinghy park are at the north end of the hard.

Hamble village proper is well worth a stroll.
Most of it is up-river from the hard, though its
pretty village green – a picnic spot – is near by,
reached via a steep rise to the south. A road
leads across Hamble Common to the Point,
where there is a marina and also 'the lair of
Cougar', who build the sort of powerboats
used by millionaire Richard Branson. It is a
great vantage point from which to view the
industrial waterside of Southampton. The
towerscape from east to west is: Calshot
coastguard tower, Fawley power station, Esso
refinery (many chimneys and a gas flare), and
in the distance Marchwood power station. To
the north, on the Hamble shore, is the ½ mile-
long pier of the BP oil terminal, opened in 1924
as a bunkering station for ships

One of the delights of Hamble is the one-
man ferry that runs throughout the year across
the mouth of the river to Warsash. It is a
pleasant way to see Hamble from the other
side and also to explore the interesting
shoreline of Warsash and Hook. On the
Warsash hard is a memorial that records the
fact that 3,000 commandos left the Hamble for
the Normandy beaches in 1944. A plaque on
the nearby Rising Sun pub says that they were
led by Brigadier Lord Lovat's personal piper.
The black-and-white tower at Warsash is the
HQ of the river's harbourmaster.

There is a pleasant walk along the whole of
the eastern bank of the Hamble estuary,
between Sarisbury Green or Swanwick in the
north, and Hook shore in the south. The
Solent Way runs east from Warsash, past the
premises of the College of Maritime Studies,
where merchant officers are trained. **Warsash**,
like Bursledon, once had an important
shipyard. Towards the end of his life George
Parsons was forced to move his yard from
Hamble to the other side of the river. A model
of one of the last ships he built, the 36-gun
frigate HMS *Hotspur*, hangs in Warsash church,

on the south-eastern outskirts of the village. This remote position was chosen in 1869 by the owner of nearby Hook Park, whose grounds are now part of the Hook-with-Warsash nature reserve. North of Warsash is Holly Hill Woodland Park, a delightful 200-acre landscaped relic of Sarisbury Court, once the home of Quintin Hogg (1845-1903), founder of the London Polytechnic, and William Garton, a Southampton brewer and proprietor of HP Sauce. The park is about a mile from the hard, but is best reached by car, via Barnes Lane.

Returning to Hamble, a visit to the parish church beside the main road (B3397) reveals other facets of this one-time fishing village. Here, near the north wall, is the grave of Sir Edwin Alliott Verdon-Roe (1877–1958), referred to as the 'first Englishman to fly', but in fact the first Englishman to fly in an all-British aircraft. He was the man who in 1916 put Hamble on the map when he set up an aircraft factory. The red shape of a Folland Gnat 1 jet fighter (built at Hamble) can be seen a mile out of the village centre. Further north, a turning to the left off the B3397 leads to Hound, which gave its name to the area until the great bulk of 'Netley Hospital', the Royal Victoria Military Hospital, started to rise on the foreshore in 1855. It came too late to help those injured in the Crimean War, but was ready for all the wars that followed. All that remains now is the green-domed chapel. This contains a permanent exhibition on the history of the hospital, which was demolished in 1966. There are fine views from the tower. The grounds of the hospital now form the Royal Victoria Country Park – ideal for picnics beside the sea amidst pine trees planted for war-weary soldiers.

To the west of the 'Royal Vic' are the substantial ruins of **Netley Abbey**, which are owned by English Heritage. It was a Cistercian house founded as an offshoot of Beaulieu. At the Dissolution it had an abbot and 12 monks.

In 1536 it was granted to Sir William Paulet of
Old Basing, who converted it into a house. It
later passed through the hands of various men,
including members of the Seymour family
(Earls of Hertford), whose main seat was at
Elvetham Hall, near Odiham. For some reason,
Netley Abbey fell into decay, to become a
celebrated picturesque ruin. Its owners
probably always saw it as a defensive site,
where fighting off French pirates was likely to
interfere with ambitions for pleasure gardens.
The remains have been stabilised and cleared
of all trees, perhaps too ruthlessly. There are
substantial remains of the church, the chapter
house and the abbot's lodging.

On the shore below the ruins is Netley
Castle, which is now a nursing home. It was
originally built in 1542 in the grounds of the
abbey as one of the Henrician forts. Paulet was
one of those in charge of the Hampshire sector
of the operation. The present form of the house
dates from about 1890, when the owner was
Sir Harry Crighton (1844–1922).

Pressures to build on the small remaining
areas of open land between Southampton and
Gosport are intense. With the exception of
Hedge End, which has grown from a village to
an industrial suburb in recent years,
development is mostly kept south of the M27.
The upper reaches of the Hamble River are
strictly preserved. The National Trust has large
areas of land at Curbridge, on the east bank.
Fairthorne Manor near by is the National
Centre of the YMCA, whilst the Upper Hamble
Country Park to the west is owned by the
county. It is reached via Junction 8 of the M27
and Pylands Lane and is an extremely pleasant
area of quiet copses, picnic areas and riverside
footpaths. Nearly 2 miles down Pylands Lane
is Manor Farm, Botley, which in 1984 became
the **Hampshire Farm Museum**. A more logical
(but unapproved) approach is via Church Lane,

Hampshire Farm Museum

William Cobbett
(1763–1835)
The main interest of
William Cobbett in the
context of Hampshire is not
only that he once lived in
the county, but that he
travelled widely and wrote
with a candour which
makes his *Rural Rides* a
unique source.

Cobbett's life was an
extraordinary one by the
standards of any age. As a
young man he went,
apparently by mistake, to
New Brunswick, Nova
Scotia, where he served for
eight years in the Canadian
army. He was so incensed
at the corruption he found
amongst the officers that on
his discharge in 1791 he
attempted to get them
court-martialled, but
instead had to flee the
country. After a short spell
in France he travelled to the
United States and made a
reputation as a journalist in
the Tory cause. In 1800 he
returned to London and
soon set up *Cobbett's Weekly
Political Register*, which he
edited until his death.

In 1806 Cobbett adopted
the Radicalism which gives
his writing such force. He
had just bought a house
and several farms at Botley
and was determined to live
the life of the country
farmer. His neighbours
must have regarded him
with some bemusement, for
he was frequently drawn to
London and elsewhere, and
between 1810 and 1812
spent two years in prison
for allegedly libelling the
government.

Oddly, his *Rural Rides*
was written in the years
immediately after he had
abandoned the country life
for Kensington.

Botley, from which a footpath runs through the
farmyard and the country park. This approach
emphasises the fact that the farm and the
church near by were once at the centre of
Botley, until new turnpikes lured the town
north.

The Hampshire Farm Museum is a
delightfully low-key affair where the emphasis
is on enjoying the traditional atmosphere of the
farm, rather than being regaled with the
minutiae of agricultural history. The farm
represents agricultural practice as it was during
the period 1850–1950, before the advent of the
tractor and intensive methods changed
everything.

The visit starts off with a video introduction
(optional) and then progresses round the yard,
which includes examples of all the traditional
sights of the farm – milking stall, granary, pig
sties, hen house, stable, pond, various barns
and the 15th-century farmhouse. With the
exception of a barn from Longstock, all the
buildings in the yard are part of the original
farm. Outside are a blacksmith's forge from
Hedge End and a wheelwright's shop from
Nether Wallop. Everything works or grunts,
for Manor Farm is still fully operational, albeit
on a small scale.

Behind the farm is the chancel of the
medieval church, where services were given by
the Botley parson, arch-enemy of that famous
local resident, radical journalist and farmer,
William Cobbett. He lived at Fairthorne Farm
(long demolished) from 1805 until about 1826
and is commemorated by a stone near the spot,
at the east end of the town, opposite the mill.
In his *Rural Rides* he recounts how the Botley
parson was once lured to London to collect a
bogus legacy. And once there he was subjected
to all manner of outrages, before he returned to
find Botley plastered with handbills telling the
yarn and offering a reward for the name of the
culprit.

Botley's main street, with its fine market hall of 1848, is that of a classic small country town: pleasant to look at and nothing to do but visit the pubs (and why not?). The great Botley Beer Jug, which can be seen in the farm museum, is one of the town's heirlooms. It may have seen action at meetings of the Botley and South Hants Farmers' Club (founded in 1844), which met monthly at the Dolphin Hotel and was an influential organisation in its day.

One of the odd facts about this part of south Hampshire is that it is administered by the Borough of **Eastleigh**. This stretches from Eastleigh town itself to the coast, taking in the west bank of the Hamble River. The borough is scarcely 50 years old and started from humble beginnings as a railway town which grew up in the mid-1800s at the intersection of two lines. This was called Bishopstoke Junction after the small village on the east bank of the river. In 1891 the London and South-Western Railway Company moved its carriage works to Eastleigh from London and in 1910 the locomotive works followed. This sealed the fate of the town and railway engineering remained its mainstay until the 1960s. The works are now used only for BR maintenance. Pirelli, who make undersea cables and much else, are also a major local employer.

The Eastleigh story is told with great style in a museum housed in a former Salvation Army Citadel in High Street.

In recent years Eastleigh has watered down its railway town image and concentrated on new businesses attracted by its position near 'Solent City' and Southampton Airport (sometimes called Eastleigh Airport). Prototype Spitfires were flown from here in the late 1930s; perhaps one of these lovely aircraft should be included in the borough's arms. Another candidate for inclusion would be the bandstand of 1903, which adds great character to the centre of the town.

Eastleigh

Population: 58,914

Early Closing: Wed

Market Day: Thu

Cashpoints: *Barclays* 20/24 Upper Market St; *Lloyds* 36 Market St; *Midland* 3 Leigh Rd; *NatWest* 34 Southampton Rd

Tourist Information: Town Hall Centre, Leigh Road

Leisure: Fleming Park Leisure Centre, Fleming Park Golf Course (municipal)

By Road: London 73 miles (A33, M3) Winchester 9 miles (A33), Southampton 6 miles (A335)

By Rail: 1hr 10mins from London (Waterloo to Weymouth line). Direct services to Fareham, Portsmouth, Southampton and Winchester

Eastleigh has a compact, modern shopping centre and has begun to exploit its position on the banks of the River Itchen. A new country park with hundreds of acres of woodland and water meadow has recently been opened. Access is from Allington Lane. To the west of the town is the sports centre and swimming pool, opened in 1975, and the extensive turf of Fleming Park. This was acquired in 1928 from the North Stoneham Estate and takes its name from the family who acquired it in about 1600. A golf course now occupies most of the old parkland of **North Stoneham**, which is hemmed in by the airport, the M27 and Eastleigh itself. North Stoneham has an exceptionally interesting, and pleasantly remote church which is reached from Eastleigh via Passfield Avenue (beside the sports centre) and then right and left into Stoneham Lane. The battlemented tower of the church has a one-hand clock and, to avoid any misunderstanding, says so, in large letters.

The church contains some fascinating memorials, including the grand tomb of Sir Thomas Fleming (1544–1613) and his wife. Dressed up to the nines, they lie propped up on their elbows. He was Chief Justice of England and as such was the man who sentenced Guy Fawkes to death. There is a much finer monument to Admiral Lord Edward Hawke (1708–1781), who in 1759 defeated the French off the Brittany coast, at Quiberon Bay. The battle is minutely depicted in the piece. He lived at nearby Swaythling but died elsewhere. Perhaps of greatest interest is a monument on the chancel floor which refers (in Italian) to 'Slavonian' sailors from what is now Yugoslavia. They died in 1491 and came from one of the Italian city states whose merchants had for centuries brought their galley fleets to Southampton to trade. They stopped coming in the 1530s, after which Southampton's fortunes took a nosedive for 300 years.

To the east of North Stoneham is the old village of **Chilworth**, now a posh residential area, where the Fleming family went to live at the turn of the century. The manor house they built is generally regarded as a mess, architecturally, though it has fine grounds. Since 1984 it has been the centrepiece of the Chilworth Research Centre, a science park where researchers from Southampton University and elsewhere try to turn bright ideas into money spinners. Chilworth church of 1812 has some intriguing plaster vaulting and contains a relief self-portrait of R C Lucas (1800–83), an eccentric sculptor who built himself a 'Tower of the Winds' (now demolished) in the village. He carved a relief in stone of one of the Flemings, which can be seen in North Stoneham church, and also one, in wax, of the businessman Charles Benny (1793–1870), which is in Winchester City Museum.

The two Stonehams, north and south, have a special place in the history of Southampton. Their names are thought to reflect the fact that they were part of a large Saxon estate which included the *stone*-built Roman fort of Clausentum, now under the modern suburb of Bitterne. Just as North Stoneham church is an intriguing villagey relic in the midst of modernity, so **South Stoneham** church is now on the edge of urban Swaythling (and alongside halls of residence of the university). It is in fact a very old minster church that once had a parish that spread to Hedge End, Botley and Eastleigh (rather like Titchfield). South Stoneham House nearby was originally built in 1708 for naval hydrographer Edmund Dummer by the famous architect Nicholas Hawksmoor, though it has been much altered.

To the south-east of the church is Woodmill, once renowned as a salmon fishery and also used by the block-maker Walter Taylor (1734–1803) in the 18th century. A pleasant footpath leads from the old mill along the east side of the River Itchen to Cobden Bridge in the south and to Mansbridge in the north. Near the latter are the works of the Ford Motor Company (best seen from the M27), the 'home of the Transit van'. The site was originally used for making aircraft and then motor bodies before Ford took it over in 1958. Southampton almost became Ford's main works when the American company decided to set up in Britain after World War I. A waterside site had been bought at Millbrook Marsh, but local freeholders demanded too high prices for adjacent mudland and foreshore rights. Southampton's loss, when the city was trying to diversify, was Dagenham's gain! But perhaps Southampton fared better.

The name **Mansbridge** refers to the surviving hump-backed bridge that was one of the key crossings of south Hampshire until modern times. The route from Fareham to the West Country once had to pass over bridges at Titchfield, Botley, Mansbridge and Redbridge. The relatively recent development of the Solent hinterland owes much to bridges built nearer to the sea, namely Bursledon and Northam Bridges, built at the end of the 18th century, and Cobden Bridge, built in 1883. The latest, and most elegant, bridge is Itchen Bridge (toll), opened in 1977 at the mouth of the river. It put the floating bridge (depicted in a well-known painting by L S Lowry) out of business.

The west side of Southampton is a mass of light industry and not very visitor-friendly until you get to Totton, which gives access to the Lower Test Nature Reserve. This beautiful area of reedland and marsh is at the start of the Test Way, which leads up to the North Hampshire Downs. The reed gave its name to Redbridge, the tiny medieval bridge which crossed the Test at the head of Southampton Water. It still stands beside the A35 and can be reached from the east-bound carriageway.

Hythe Marina

The muddy western shore of Southampton Water is called the Waterside. It is heavily industrialised, yet has large tracts of countryside and is of considerable interest. First port of call (literally) is **Eling**, to the south of Totton. This delightful little harbour has its fair share of pleasure yachts but is still tatty enough to feel like a real place. Eling tide mill is probably the only tide-driven mill still producing flour in western Europe, albeit with the aid of grants and volunteer labour. Sea water is ponded up at high water and then allowed to turn the mill-wheel as the tide falls. There are two mill-stones set side-by-side, but only one has been restored to working order. The mill is regularly open to view and its 'Canute' brand of flour is on sale. This superb restoration job has kept alive a type of mill that once was relatively common around the coast.

Eling church is basically medieval, but it was drastically restored in the last century. It contain many fine monuments but the most interesting is probably the tombstone of William Mansbridge, who died in 1703, which relates that 'theivs by night when in my bed/ Broak up my house and shot me dead'. *Plus ça change*! A footpath leads from the churchyard to the foreshore, which is an excellent vantage point for viewing shipping and the container port.

Quiet country roads lead from Eling to **Hythe**, (which can also be reached from Southampton by ferry). The route passes the towering chimney of Marchwood power station, which is mothballed, and the yards of Marchwood military port. This is devoted to the less glamorous side of fighting wars. *Sir Galahad*, the transport sunk in the Falklands war, came from here. A nearby salty spot worth seeking is **Cracknore Hard**, to the south of the power station. Binocular buffs will find heavy ship traffic and the sights of the western and eastern docks. To the south is a large area

Tide mills
The resurgence of interest in alternative sources of power in recent years makes the principle of the tide mill look rather modern. The basic idea is to trap water in a tidal estuary at high tide and then to allow it to flow out via a waterwheel until the flood tide has started again. As the time of high tide varies from day to day, the life of the tide-miller is, to say the least, an antisocial one, with a continous cyclical change from day-shift to night-shift, and everything in between.

Eling tide mill appears to have been in existence at the time of Domesday Book. It later came into the hands of Winchester College, which held it until recent years. It is said to be the only mill surviving anywhere in the world that still harnesses the power of the tides for the regular production of flour. It was reopened in 1980 after extensive restoration. It has two sets of millstones, each separately driven, but only one has been restored to working order. The water wheels at Eling were cast in iron and installed by Armfields of Ringwood at the beginning of the century. There were once other tide mills on the Hampshire coast at Ashlett, Beaulieu, Fareham, Langstone, Emsworth and elsewhere.

Hampshire oilfields

When Fawley oil refinery was started by the Atlantic Gulf and West Indies Petroleum Company in 1921 it obtained all its feedstocks from Mexico. It was located near Southampton because there were facilities for tankers and because one of its main purposes was to provide fuel oil for shipping. Another oil bunkering terminal was set up in 1924 at Hamble.

The notion that crude oil might be available locally was not seriously considered by the oil companies. All that has now changed: oil is pumped to the surface from Jurassic strata 1,500m beneath the surface. The BP terminal at Hamble has just completed a direct pipeline feed from the oilfield at Wytch Farm, near Poole.

The main oilfields centre on Stockbridge, Horndean and Humbly Grove, a tiny hamlet 5 miles north of Alton. Humbly Grove is in production and oil will soon start to flow from the Stockbridge field. At Humbly Grove, developed by Carless Exploration, the crude oil is separated on site from gas and water and then transported to a terminal on the Alton–Farnham railway. The boreholes of the Stockbridge field, an Amoco project, extend over a large area between Waller's Ash and Chilbolton.

Despite considerable local opposition, the oil business has now become part of the Hampshire landscape.

of reclaimed land awaiting bright ideas. Once such idea has already been put into action at Hythe, where in 1984 the local resident and hovercraft inventor, Sir Christopher Cockerell, laid the first brick of a novel marina village. Lock gates allow yachts to move, at all states of the tide, in and out of a two-basin marina, where residents can literally tie up at their back door. An attractive canal-like bridge separates the two pools and a perky village centre faces down the central channel. There is a chandlery, a few shops and the Lock 'n' Quay pub (ugh!). The street names echo the names of great yachts, like *Endeavour* and *Shamrock*. The design of the place is superb and in high summer it must be idyllic. Although the marina village looks very private, most of it is open to the public and there is a public slipway. Opposite are the great grain silos of Southampton's eastern docks.

The Waterside shore is for mudlarks, not swimmers. But there is a large pool and other facilities at the Applemore Recreation Centre (turn left at the Applemore roundabout on the A326). Also a variety of sports facilites (but no swimming), and pleasant grassland round a small lake, can be found at the Gang Warily Recreation Centre (south of Fawley oil refinery). Its name ('go carefully') is taken from the arms of the Drummond family, who once owned all the land hereabouts. Opposite the pierhead of Hythe stands the stately Drummond Arms, which takes its name from Robert Drummond, the Scots-born banker who in 1772 bought an estate stretching almost the entire length of the Waterside. It was called the Cadland Estate, after the manor at the southernmost tip, where gravel cliffs above a secluded shore face the Isle of Wight. His descendants still live there, in a house designed as seaside cottage by Henry Holland with grounds landscaped by 'Capability' Brown.

Hythe is a pleasant place with modern shopping centre. Its lifeline is the ferry to Southampton, which 'steps over' the mudlands by leaving from a very long pier. Hythe Pier is in fact almost ½ mile long and the journey to the pontoon is made in a small electric train.

The mansion house of the Cadland Estate once stood in the middle of what is now the Esso oil refinery at **Fawley**. Originally a place where crude oil came in by ship and petrol left in cans, it has long had pipelines that take its products to London and the Midlands.

Esso have made great efforts to conceal the plant with belts of trees, but 'gassy' smells occasionally pervade the neighbourhood. The pipes and tanks and chimneys of the works (most dramatic at night) can best be seen from the south, from the approaches to Fawley village. To the south is **Ashlett**, a charming place with a tiny harbour, green, pub, tide mill (now an Esso social club) and quay. A footpath (accompanied by a prominent pipeline) leads from the harbour, alongside Fawley power station (oil-fired, of course) to **Calshot**, a small place which was put on the map when it became a station for seaplanes (hence its Flying Boat pub) just before World War I. The runway was Southampton Water and the main base on Calshot Spit, at the extreme tip of the Waterside. It remained an air station until 1961 (the planes flew until 1958).

Nearly 400 years earlier, in 1539, the spit was chosen as the site for one of the shore-defence castles ordered by Henry VIII. The original castle, with later additions, still stands at the end of the spit, overshadowed by a tall coastguard tower. It is a small castle, owned by English Heritage, and contains a display on the history of the spit. Originally a naval air station, it became famous in 1928 and 1931, when it was the base for the Schneider Races. In 1928 the British pilot. Lt G L Brinton, was

Flying boats over the Solent

Calshot, Hythe, Hamble and Southampton were centres of flying boat activities that continued locally until 1958. The convenience of being able to take off or land on any stretch of water attracted the Admiralty. In March 1913 they designated Calshot one of a chain of coastal air stations. Later, Hythe became a maintenance centre and Hamble was involved in testing new aircraft.

From 1913, floatplanes were made locally, on the Isle of Wight, at Cowes, where the boatbuilders John Samuel White and S E Saunders (later Saunders-Roe) put traditional skills to new use. Sopwith Aviation also came briefly to the Itchen to build flying boats at Woolston, where Noel Pemberton-Billing was founding the Supermarine Aviation Company.

In the early 1920s Southampton became an important marine airport notably under Imperial Airways, later part of BOAC. In the 1930s services went to Newfoundland, Karachi, Singapore, Hong Kong and elsewhere. In 1948 Southampton Marine Airport seemed set for a rosy future. A luxurious new terminal had just been opened in the Eastern Docks. But within two years BOAC decided to cease all flying boat services from here.

Some services were taken on by Aquila Airways, a small firm that operated until 1958.

Solent shores

The western side of
Southampton Water
contains a large area of
mudflats and saltmarshes of
international importance.
Eling Great Marsh is
grazed, which makes it an
ideal habitat for some rare
grasses and fescues.

The shore ecology of the
Solent area has been
affected dramatically by the
transatlantic traffic of
Southampton Docks. Not
only did this bring alien
species of shellfish,
including the quahog or
American clam, but also a
species of marine grass or
Spartina which interbred
with local species to
produce a vigorous hybrid.
This trapped mud in its
roots and created large
areas of mudbank.
Curiously, the hybrid is
now dying back and coastal
erosion is removing land
that *Spartina* has reclaimed.

Much of the Solent
shore is made up of shingle
which is so frequently
trodden that nothing can
grow on it. However, the
beaches of the North Solent
Reserve between Calshot
and the Beaulieu river show
that it can, in fact, support
a natural flora, consisting of
such plants as sea kale,
little robin, yellow horned
poppy, sea campion and
thrift.

killed. His grave is in Fawley churchyard. 'Re-
enactments' of the races and other enthusiast
events are staged occasionally.

·The tip of Calshot Spit, which is virtually
surrounded by water, is a fascinating place to
visit in its own right. There is no better place
from which to view the ships entering and
leaving Southampton Water, for the deep-
water channel passes alongside the castle. The
former buildings of RAF Calshot are now used
by the Calshot Activities Centre, the largest
centre of its kind in the country. It has a dry
ski slope and many other facilities and is used
by children from Hampshire schools and by
local residents. The rather gaunt shapes of the
old hangars have been cleverly broken up by
huge colourful sail-shaped murals.

The shingle beach on the south side of the
spit is popular with bathers and windsurfers.
There is a pleasant walk along the shore to the
edge of the North Solent Nature Reserve,
which is not open to the general public. The
route passes beneath Luttrell's Tower, a folly
built in the 1780s and since 1968 owned by the
Landmark Trust, a charitable organisation
which rents it as holiday accommodation. It
has extensive cellars and a passage to the
beach. This was one of the places from which
Marconi demonstrated that radio waves could
travel across water, to the Isle of Wight. He
stayed at nearby Eaglehurst, orginally the
Luttrell house. It later became a camp for the
seaplane station. A small train, nicknamed the
'Calshot Express', ran between house and spit.

About two miles to the south-west of
Calshot is **Lepe Country Park**, actually a *seaside*
park. It stands at Stone Point and is reached
from Calshot by doubling back towards Fawley
and taking the first turning left. As already
mentioned, the foreshore between Calshot and
Lepe is a reserve and not open to the public.
Lepe Country Park is an ideal place to park the
car and laze away the day. There is a sandy

beach and plenty to occupy birdwatchers.
Distant views of the Gurnard shores on the Isle
of Wight back a steady traffic of yachts and
ships. A pleasant footpath leads along the
shore to the marshy approaches to the Beaulieu
River, and to Lower Exbury. This is one of the
least spoilt parts of the Hampshire coast.

Hardy walkers can continue to the north, to
Exbury, though the village is easily reached
from Lepe by road. Here are Exbury Gardens,
world-famous for their rhododendrons. They
were created between the wars by the money
of Lionel de Rothschild, who was said to have
been 'a banker by hobby, a gardener by
profession'. His descendants still live in the
house he bought and neo-Georgianised in
1919. He converted 250 acres of mostly virgin
forest into garden and planted thousands of
varieties of plants. When complete, it required
a staff of 75 who used 22 miles of underground
piping for watering. Much of 'Mr Lionel's'
garden still remains. Each year in early
summer it erupts into a mass of colour. There
is also a plant centre, where many of the
thousand or more crosses made at Exbury can
be bought. The main emphasis is on
rhododendrons, azaleas and camellias, but
there are also pieris and cotoneasters, and
many species of trees. The story of the garden
is told by a video, with commentary by James
Mason.

Exbury is a small sedate village which in its
present position dates only from 1827. The
present church contains a Purbeck marble font
of about 1200 which probably came from the
old church. Although originally built in 1827,
the present church dates mostly from 1909,
when extensive alterations were made. There
is a memorial chapel to two sons of Lord Forster
(1866–1936) who were killed during World War
I. He was the owner of Exbury House before
Lionel de Rothschild and a Governor General
of Australia.

Luttrell's Tower, Calshot

4 New Forest, the Avon Valley and the Martin Peninsula

The south-west corner of Hampshire is largely taken up by the New Forest, a vast area of outstandingly beautiful heath and woodland protected for more than 900 years.

There are few large towns. Places like Lyndhurst, Brockenhurst, Lymington and Ringwood are important not because they are sizable but because they provide everyday services in an area of open countryside. It is a fantastic place for walkers and naturalists – within easy reach of the M3 and M27 motorways and yet wonderfully peaceful. The forest stretches to the shores of the Solent, which include the North Solent Nature Reserve between Cadland and Beaulieu, the yacht-jammed harbour of Lymington and the clifflands of Christchurch Bay. A 16-mile leg of the 60-mile Solent Way runs from Milford-on-Sea to Buckler's Hard, and on to Hythe and Southampton.

To the west of the region, just outside the statutory boundary of the forest, flows the 'Hampshire' Avon, which in its middle section acts as the border between Hampshire and Dorset and further south runs entirely within Dorset.

The arrow-shaped Martin Peninsula in the northwest, sandwiched between Dorset and Wiltshire, includes pretty villages, and miles of fine, open chalkland. It takes in Martin Down, now a National Nature Reserve, which was celebrated in W H Hudson's *A Shepherd's Life*. It is part of Cranborne Chase, which continues to the west.

Most people visiting this part of the county make for the New Forest, which attracts huge numbers of people each year. The crowds are not hard to escape: the forest is large enough to absorb the hordes, whilst plenty of small free car parks are provided everywhere.

LYNDHURST AND THE NEW FOREST

The first-time visitor to the New Forest should make for the Museum and Visitor Centre, which adjoins the main car park in Lyndhurst. Here will be found a comprehensive account of the New Forest, from 1079, when William the Conqueror designated the area his *nova foresta*, to the present day. The annual New Forest Show provides a good opportunity to see all aspects of the forest at work and play – and a lot more. It is held in the summer at New Park, between Lyndhurst and Brockenhurst.

The capital of the forest is **Lyndhurst**, a pleasant small town, once called 'the most aristocratic in England', which is contained within a triangle of three busy roads. Most of the shops and restaurants are in the High Street. To the east lies a pleasant area of open grassland, where a game of cricket is often in progress. Here also is Bolton's Bench, named after a 17th-century Lord Warden of the forest, and also a cemetery where John Wise, historian of the forest, lies buried.

At the west end of High Street stands the Queen's House, a royal manor house of mainly Stuart vintage which is now occupied by the Forestry Commission. It includes the Verderers Courtroom, which dates from 1388. Alongside is the parish church, a fascinating exercise in Victorian brick Gothic. It evokes the countrified feeling of the forest and is at the same time artistically exciting. It contains glass by Edward Burne-Jones and other Pre-Raphaelites. A huge fresco beneath the east window was painted in 1864 by Frederick Leighton, the first painter to be raised to the peerage. The ashes of Mrs Reginald Hargreaves, who was the living model for Lewis Carroll's Alice in Wonderland and at one time lived in Lyndhurst, are buried in the family vault to the south of the church.

Government of the forest
The routine business of the New Forest is looked after by an ancient court, i.e. a court similar to a manorial court. The governing body has ten members (called verderers), of whom one is appointed by the crown and four others by various public bodies (Hampshire County Council, Forestry Commission, Ministry of Agriculture and the Countryside Commission). The five remaining verderers are elected by the commoners of the forest. The court meets in open session, in an ancient courthouse in Lyndhurst, six times per annum.

A key function of the court is to regulate the activities of the animals set loose on the forest by the commoners. With the assistance of four full-time keepers (called agisters), the animals are carefully monitored and controlled. Each animal is branded with the mark of its owner and its tail is cropped and notched in a particular way to indicate the agisterial area to which it belongs. The agisters dress formally in green livery with leather gaiters and have the mark of a stirrup on their riding hats.

In the late summer and autumn, the agisters and commoners round up the animals in 'drifts'. Those which are to be sold are presented at a series of sales held at Beaulieu Road, to the east of Lyndhurst.

The nature of the forest

The New Forest owes it existence to the fact that its soils were too poor to attract farmers. But its special status has been maintained by careful management, and by statute. It was originally a royal hunting preserve subject to forest law (though some of its lands have long been privately owned). Since 1923 it has been under the care of the Forestry Commission.

Much of the special character of the forest is due to the fact that most of it is unenclosed and uncultivated. Its wide grassy verges and open commons are now unique in the south of England: they are reminders of what the countryside must have looked like elsewhere before wholesale enclosure. The heathes, bogs and woodlands of the forest depend on a subtle balance between man and nature. The wild deer, and particularly the ponies and cattle, are critical, because without them the forest would literally 'go wild'. Most of the forest consists of 'dry and humid heath' (20,000 acres), with substantial expanses of enclosed conifers (12,000 acres) and 'traditional' broadleaved woodlands (9,000 acres).

The forest has a unique flora and fauna, with a remarkable number of rare species of interest to specialists. Amongst its rarities are the honey buzzard, the hobby and the European tree frog.

The A35 road to Bournemouth leads from Lyndhurst to **Swan Green**, a pretty spot with thatched cottages around a cricket green. Two miles further on, on the north side of the road, is Holidays Hill camp site, where the Forestry Commission have set up a public reptiliary. Here the snakes and lizards of the forest live and breed naturally in low-walled cells. It is fascinating watching on a warm sunny day, when snakes sun themselves and climb trees. The next turning to the right leads to the Knightwood Oak, which is reckoned to be nearly 400 years old and as such is the oldest pollarded oak tree in the forest. It stands near the Bolderwood Ornamental Drive, which leads after 3 miles to several car parks alongside waymarked paths.

To the north of Lyndhurst lies the pleasant village of **Minstead**. Sir Arthur Conan Doyle and his wife are buried in the churchyard. At one time they lived to the north of the old parish at Bignells Wood. The church itself is a charming cottagey building, which still has a three-decker pulpit and two tiers of galleries, where minstrels once played and gypsies were tolerated. The village's Trusty Servant pub takes its name from a strange painting of a man with an ass's head. The original hangs in Winchester College. Furzey Gardens in Minstead cover eight acres of rare and beautiful plants, from exotic azaleas to Chilean fire trees.

The famous Rufus Stone, where William II was killed, stands to the north of Minstead (but must be reached from Cadnam or Bolderwood as the A31 cannot be crossed from the south). To this day there is still a mystery surrounding the death of this king. No one knows whether it was a hunting accident, a power coup, a killing for love or even a ritual killing. The nearby Sir Walter Tyrrell pub is named after the man who probably loosed the fatal arrow and escaped afterwards on a boat which is said to have been waiting for him at Lymington.

A minor road leads from the Rufus Stone to the hamlets of Fritham and Eyeworth, which are amongst the prettiest places in the forest. The pond at Eyeworth is a delight, but a man-made one with a violent background. It was created by damming in about 1870, when a German national by the name of Captain Schultze decided to set up a gunpowder factory at this remote location. The works made use of local charcoal, which was one of the traditional products of the forest until modern times. The rude huts where the burners lived could be found in many parts of the forest (the craft is demonstrated at the Weald and Downland Museum at Singleton, near Chichester.)

One unashamedly 'unnatural' tourist attraction is the New Forest Butterfly Farm, which in fact stands outside the forest, near Ashurst. Less imaginative but in some ways more unusual is the nearby Longdown Dairy Farm, which is a fully operational farm open to the public. Ideal for city folk who have forgotten where the milk comes from (or never knew!).

Beaulieu

The red coronets that surmount the boundary marks of the Beaulieu Estate are reminders that you are entering private property. Not that it feels like that: the Palace House and the National Motor Museum are a professional tourist attraction created by Lord Montagu of Beaulieu, who can fairly lay claim to being a pioneer of the stately home business.

It all started in 1952, the year after Lord Montagu inherited the estate (and three years before Woburn opened), when he opened the Palace House to visitors and placed a few veteran cars in the hall as an attraction. The collection grew. Vintage models were soon being kept in every spare corner at Beaulieu. Twenty years later this unique collection became housed in the custom-built premises of

Commoners and enclosures
Ancient rights of common are attached to particular lands in the New Forest. These rights enable land owners to turn out their cattle and ponies into the forest, an arrangement which once ensured the livelihood of the commoner whilst at the same time allowing royal huntsmen unfettered access in the chase. Subsequently, when the forest acquired more value as a source of timber, the crown wanted to enclose land.

The first enclosures (of doubtful legality) were made by Charles II in about 1670. An Act of 1698 and successive statutes accommodated new needs as they arose. The enclosure of land was not, of course, in the interests of commoners, which inevitably led to a certain tension between them and the authorities. In the middle of the last century attempts were made to clear the forest of deer and to enclose vast tracts of land for timber production (only a few years before the admiralty started to build iron ships!). This prompted a vigorous local protest and led to the formation of the New Forest Association, one of the country's oldest conservation pressure groups. However, although there are constant pressures from oil exploration companies and others to use parts of the forest, the greatest threat comes from the fact that 'commuter' commoners no longer wish to own animals. And no grazing means no forest – or a very different one.

Beaulieu Abbey

In 1204 King John granted 10,000 acres of land within the New Forest to a Cistercian community. It was the only religious house he ever founded. The monks originally lived in a royal hunting lodge, but they soon started to build a traditional monastic complex and by 1246 had completed a great abbey church, 336ft long. The lines of its walls can be seen on the ground. After the Dissolution, much of the abbey stone was used in the construction of the forts at Hurst, Calshot and elsewhere.

Beaulieu Abbey relied for its income on a system of grange farms worked by lay brothers. A substantial part of the 'domus' where some of them lived still survives. The refectory where the monks ate also survives and has become the parish church at Beaulieu. Its origins are reflected in its north-south alignment.

Beaulieu Abbey was at its peak in the second half of the 13th century. The Black Death affected its economy by increasing the cost of labour. It briefly played a part on the national stage when in 1497 Perkin Warbeck, pretender to the throne, sought sanctuary there after his farcical attempt to take the English throne.

At the Dissolution the abbey and its lands were sold to Thomas Wriothesley (1505–50), from whom it has descended to the present owner, the 3rd Baron Montagu of Beaulieu.

the National Motor Museum. It includes everything from the humble 1923 Austin Seven Chummy to Donald Campbell's 4-ton Bluebird, which reached 403.1 mph in 1964. The oldest exhibit, and probably the first petrol-driven car to run on British public roads, is the pioneering 1895 Knight with tiller steering, which a Farnham engineer invented. There is enough in the Museum to keep an enthusiast quiet for hours, or even days.

There is much else to do at Beaulieu, from the pure fun of riding on a monorail or a miniature veteran car, to viewing the Palace House itself or the ruins of the abbey. This is where the Beaulieu story really started in 1204, when King John gave land in the forest to a community of monks. The remains of the huge tithe barn used by them for storing grain on one of the granges still stand at St Leonards, to the west of the entrance of the Beaulieu River.

Two miles below the abbey ruins is **Buckler's Hard** a gem of a place, an almost unspoilt 18th-century estate village. It can be reached from the centre of Beaulieu village by road or via a fine riverside path. Buckler's Hard was a shipyard until 1822. A total of 55 ships were built here for the Admiralty, including vessels up to 74 guns and Nelson's favourite, the *Agamemnon*. The story of shipbuilding on the site is told in a Maritime Museum, which also includes relics from the voyages of single-handed yachtsman Sir Francis Chichester (1901–1972), who moored his boats on the river.

The wide street of this one-street village, which was once piled up with forest timber, still echoes with the ghosts of the men who worked here. If you do not feel their presence in the master builder's house, you are bound to meet them in the reconstructed New Inn, where the enterprising Lord Montagu has set up a reconstruction of the public bar and its locals, complete with authentic smells and taped conversations.

The Beaulieu River is the only unspoilt waterway on the Solent. It is best seen aboard the *Swiftsure*, named after the 76-gun vessel launched in 1804, which regularly cruises from Buckler's Hard to the entrance of the river and the fringes of the North Solent Nature Reserve.

Brockenhurst

When the railway brought Victorian tourists to the Forest in 1847 it turned Brockenhurst from a tiny village into a small town. Eventually the junction to the south of the village carried lines to Lymington, Bournemouth and Ringwood.

The part of Brockenhurst which most people see first is probably the grand Balmer Lawn Hotel, which stands beside the upper reaches of the Lymington River. Balmer Lawn is an extensive area of typical streamside New Forest greensward. The river nearby has become the New Forest's unofficial 'paddling pool', albeit one that is said to be badly polluted.

The shopping centre of Brockenhurst is on the west side of the A337 Lyndhurst road. The main street is Brookley Road, which from the north is reached via a ford called the Watersplash. Most eateries and drinkeries are alongside the A337, including the Snakecatcher pub and the Morant Arms pub, which takes its name from the men who were lords of the manor. They lived at Brockenhurst Park, which still exists in the older part of the village, on the east side of the A337. A fine French-style gatehouse survives in Mill Lane.

Brockenhurst church, which is also on the east side of the road, was the only forest church recorded in Domesday Book (though Boldre church was probably also in existence). It is noted for the grave of 'Brusher' Mills (1840–1905), the legendary snakecatcher. His finely carved tombstone stands to the north of the church, near a mass of military graves.

Snakes and snakecatchers
Every native British species of reptile can be found in the New Forest. As well as the common adder, there are also breeding populations of smooth snake and a few sand lizards.

The reptiles are protected, but vipers were once caught to supply zoos. The most celebrated snakecatcher was 'Brusher' Mills, who for 19 years lived in a disused charcoal burner's hut. First he would trap the snake with a forked stick and then lift it into a sack by means of long tongs with flattened ends. After his death in 1905, the tools of his trade and his contract with the London Zoo went to a Lyndhurst forester.

'Brusher' Mills's tomb

Brusher made a living by supplying the
London Zoo with adders for snake-eating
animals. He also entertained Victorian
sightseers, who were eager to find local colour.

Rhinefield Road leads from the
Watersplash, past the Victorian gothic church
of St Saviour. It leads on after a couple of miles
to Rhinefield House, now a splendid hotel,
which was built on the site of an ancient lodge.
Beyond the hotel the road becomes the
Rhinefield Ornamental Drive, which is one of
the splendours of the forest. It was planted by
a nurseryman in the middle of the last century
and consists of an avenue of huge specimens of
various species of foreign trees, including a
Redwood 42 metres high, numerous Douglas
Firs, a Wellingtonia and many others. Three
way-marked paths lead from car parks. The
longest is the Tall Trees Walk, which is well
furnished with plaques explaining many
features of the forest. One records that it
supplied 12 million cubic feet of timber for the
1939–45 war, which is why the Luftwaffe made
repeated efforts to set it alight!

Fordingbridge

This has long been a major crossroads and a
convenient point at which to cross the
Hampshire Avon between Salisbury and
Ringwood. It stands entirely on the right bank
of the river, just outside the perambulation of
the New Forest, which runs a mile or two to
the east. It is a lived-in town, not prettified or
tarted-up.

There are two focal points, a villagey one
around the church, where a ford probably once
crossed the river, and a traffic-bound one
around the George Inn and the bridge, which
became the main crossing-point. This graceful
seven-arch medieval structure, the finest bridge
in the county, was widened in the last century.
There is a good view of it from the children's
playground and memorial gardens on the east
side of the river. Here also stands a rough-

hewn statue by Sir Ivor Roberts Jones of the artist Augustus John (1878–1961) in heroic pose. From 1928 until his death he lived at Upper Burgate, to the north of Fordingbridge. The memorial is tucked away by the side of the river, as if to acknowledge his reputation as a painter but to exercise some doubts about his ripe lifestyle!

The medieval church of Fordingbridge is the only one I know that is entered by plate-glass doors. Its interior shows it to be an Early English church, much expanded to accommodate the growing medieval population of the town.

The most pleasant approach to Fordingbridge is from Ringwood, along one of the two roads which flank the valley of the Hampshire Avon, particularly that to the east. This runs through South Gorley, North Gorley and other small villages on the edge of the Forest. It is striking that virtually all the villages of the Avon valley are situated some distance from the river itself, where presumably the land was too marshy. Or were they squatters' settlements? It is noticeable that the west side of the valley is virtually villageless. One exception is Harbridge, with its prominent church tower and bullbaiter's grave of 1758 (opposite the south-east corner of the tower).

On the east side of the valley is Moyles Court at **Ellingham**, which was once the home of Dame Alice Lisle, the Protestant martyr executed in 1685 for sheltering two refugees from the battle of Sedgemoor. She is buried at Ellingham church, which lies alongside the A338 Ringwood-Salisbury road. Moyles Court itself is a fine 17th-century house with stables flanking the roadside. It is now used by a private school. The Alice Lisle Inn at Rockford was also once a school.

One of the most watery places on the Avon is Bickton Mill, which can be reached via a

Earthworks of the New Forest and Heywood Sumner

Anyone who walks in the New Forest will soon notice that it is littered with 'humps and bumps' of obscure origin. Archaeological studies have shown that there are a variety of explanations for these remains. Some are simple boundary banks, others are relics of hunting lodges, boiling mounds (heaps of stones used to boil water on) or bee gardens, or the remains of Roman potteries. To the south-east of Lyndhurst, for example, are the prominent remains of the bank of a 200-acre medieval deer park. The Bishop's Dyke to the south of Beaulieu Road Station is an even more complete example of a medieval bank.

Many other earthworks of the forest invite speculation, for there are many uninterpreted structures, despite intensive efforts by archaeologists. The man who probably did more than anyone else to study them was George Heywood Sumner (1853–1940), son of Mary Sumner, who was by profession an architect and designer. At the age of 51 he moved in semi-retirement to 'Cuckoo Hill', a house of his own design at South Gorley, near Fordingbridge. At first he studied the earthworks of Cranborne Chase and then turned his attention to the New Forest. He was particularly interested in the Roman potteries of the forest.

footpath from Fordingbridge. Like Harbridge and several other places in the valley, it is the site of a deserted medieval village. This is the place to come in the late autumn to see Avon salmon fighting their way up the ladder by the mill sluices.

Near Fordingbridge is **Breamore House and Countryside Museum** (said 'Bremmer'), where an extraordinary collection of carefully curated country bygones has been set out in authentic surroundings. The workshops of the blacksmith, bootmaker, wheelwright and other village craftsmen have been recreated in loving detail. Prize exhibit of the carriage collection is the Red Rover, the last stage-coach to run between Southampton and London. This and other exhibits dramatically spell out the impact of steam and the petrol engine on rural life.

The museum also contains the 1200ft brick maze that was the winning entry in the Great British Maze competition organised in 1983 by the *Sunday Times*. On the top of Breamore Down to the north-west of the house is an ancient turf maze of unknown date.

Breamore House itself is a fine Elizabethan E-shaped country house that was rebuilt after a fire of 1856. Since the late 17th century it has been the home of the Hulse family. It was built in 1583 by William Dodington, who later committed suicide, very publicly, by throwing himself from a Holborn church.

Breamore church is an outstanding example of a Saxon church built in the century before the Norman Conquest. Seven Saxon double-splayed windows still sit in its massive flint walls. The arch of the south transept carries a rare example of a Saxon inscription that translates as: 'Here the covenant is explained to thee.' A dozen hatchments (funereal arms) hang high up on the walls of the crossing: I have never seen so many in one church!

Worth a detour in this astonishingly rich and unspoilt corner of Hampshire are the

Saxon church, Breamore

murals which adorn the walls of the village hall of Wood Green, a mile to the south-east of Breamore.

Hale church, which stands above the River Avon to the north of Wood Green, is an early 17th-century building with Classical additions by Thomas Archer (d.1743) the architect, who probably also designed nearby Hale House (not open to the public). The avenue of trees in front of the house runs for almost a mile to Hatchet Green, a delightful spot which, until 1975, when it was vested in the parish council, had no known owner.

To the east of Breamore, reached by wooded winding lanes, stands **Rockbourne Roman Villa**, which is said to be the largest of its kind in the country. It was discovered by a ferreter in 1942 and privately acquired and excavated by a local estate agent, A T Morley Hewitt. It is now owned by the county and recently had its small museum revamped. On show are examples of New Forest Ware, the characteristic local pottery made during the Roman period.

A short distance from the villa site stands a lofty monument. This commemorates Major General Sir Eyre Coote (1726–83), a distinguished soldier of his day whose exploits helped to establish imperial rule in India in the 18th century. He came to live at West Park in Rockbourne village, which is an extremely pretty place strung out along a winterbourne. The centre of the old village lies off the road, to the east of the Rose and Thistle pub and is well worth a visit. A fascinating complex of manorial medieval buildings lies beneath an ornate church where Eyre Coote fans can have a field day. He died at Madras.

Rockbourne is part of the **Martin Peninsula**, an odd arrow-shaped westerly projection of Hampshire which juts out above Fordingbridge. It is an area of pretty villages and pleasant chalk downland, part of which, to the west of Martin village, is preserved as a National Nature Reserve. This is walking country of the highest order. Martin Down was trod by Caleb Bawcombe, the real-life shepherd of W H Hudson's *A Shepherd's Life*. The old man told all he knew to the author, who captured a way of life that is now long dead.

Lymington

Boats, boats and more boats. This is the main industry of this affluent little town. Two yachtsmen who use its harbour won a Gold Medal in the Star Class of the 1988 Seoul Olympics. Commercial fishing boats, expensive yachts, swans and the general maritime clutter of the harbour all blend together in a scene which has delighted many an artist. Quay Hill and Quay Street still have the character of the old port that was once Lymington. The former customs house of 1680 survives on the east side of Quay Street.

Lymington lies entirely on the right-hand side of the estuary of its river. It is the terminus of a rail-boat service to Yarmouth on the Isle of Wight, which makes a most enjoyable excursion. The main street of the town, 'blocked off' at the top by the church, has changed little since the 18th century, when it became a popular venue with the well-to-do. The High Street has been the site of a market since the 12th century. Each Saturday it is lined with an enormous variety of stalls. Some of the permanent shops also have a long continuous history of trading by one family, including King's Bookshop, founded in 1735, and Klitz's Music Shop, started 54 years later by a Bavarian émigré.

A recent addition to the local scene is Lymington Vineyard, which was started in 1979 and offers *dégustation* to passers-by. There are also vineyards at Ringwood and Lyndhurst. Lymington's six acres of vines are on the south side of Wainsford Road, Pennington, a 15-minute walk from the High Street.

Until the middle of the last century Lymington's main industry was extracting salt from sea water. Remains of the 'chocolate square' salterns can still be seen alongside a delightful path (part of the Solent Way) that runs around the western side of the estuary to Keyhaven and beyond. It follows a long curving sea-wall that protects the marshes of Pennington and Keyhaven, which are famous in birdwatching circles. Large numbers of wintering birds from Iceland, northern Scandinavia and Russia live here throughout the autumn and winter months.

Keyhaven itself is a delightful tiny harbour with little more than a couple of sailing clubs, a cluster of cottages and the Gun Inn. It was once the haunt of Colonel Peter Hawker (1786–1853), an aptly named Test Valley sportsman who killed vast numbers of wildfowl in the area in the first half of the last century. During the summer months a regular ferry runs from Keyhaven to Hurst Castle, which stands half a mile from the shore at the end of a great shingle pit. It is managed by English Heritage. Around the central Tudor castle built by Henry VIII is wrapped a much larger Victorian fort. Charles I perforce spent some time here on his final journey to London from Carisbrooke Castle on the Isle of Wight. Hardy walkers might like to 'yomp' back to the shore along the shingle spit. This is quite safe but tougher than it looks!

This leg of the Solent Way continues to **Milford-on-Sea**, which is a modest resort dating from 1887. It stands at the east end of Christchurch Bay, which, as its name suggests, curves round as far as the famous priory town of Christchurch (part of Hampshire until 1974). This is a part of the coast where ironstone was once collected by cart, for use at an ironworks at Sowley, two miles to the east of Lymington.

Barton-on-Sea is another small resort like

Salt and salterns

Salt is still extracted from the sea in warmer climes, but in England the practice has entirely died out. The name 'Salterns Lane' or the like often gives a clue to an area that was involved in making salt. In Hampshire alone the name can be found at several places, including Bursledon, Hayling Island and Fareham.

It was a seasonal business, carried out only in the summer, when large areas of shallow salt water, called pans, could be partially evaporated by the sun. The liquor was then concentrated further by boiling, when the salt and other minerals (Epsom and Glauber salts) crystallised out.

There were about a dozen places in Hampshire with salt pans at the time of Domesday. Major areas in later periods included the east side of Portsea Island, Milford-on-Sea and Lymington. At its peak Lymington was producing about 6,000 tons per annum, which was one-tenth of the nation's output of salt. The business at Lymington gradually declined over the years, until the last pan ceased production in 1865. Heavy salt taxes contributed to the demise of the southern salterns, but competition from mined Cheshire salt spelt its end.

Milford. Pleasant for a sit and a stare at the busy sea lanes of the Needles and the Solent, with a view that stretches from Hurst to Hengistbury Head, site of an Iron Age port. Its slumpy gravelly cliffs offer rich pickings for fossil hunters (and can be dangerous). The fossils of the Christchurch Bay area were first studied by Gustavus Brander in his classic work of 1776. The Barton Beds are used by geologists to define the Eocene division of the Tertiary Strata.

The adjacent village of New Milton has a modern swimming pool and leisure centre in Gore Road. Nearby is Sammy Miller's museum of motor-cycles, which boasts one of the world's largest collection of historic machines, including 'the first bike to lap a Grand Prix course at over 100 mph'. A striking landmark in this part of Hampshire is the 218ft Peterson's Tower, which stands about half a mile south of the road between New Milton and **Sway**. Hereabouts stood Arnewood House, which was the setting for Captain Marryat's famous story, *The Children of the New Forest*.

A turning off the A337 Lyndhurst–Brockenhurst road leads east to **Boldre** (say 'Bolder'), which is a scattered forest village made famous by Rev William Gilpin (1724–1804), whose writings on landscape did much to form the views of late 18th-century taste. The pretty church he served is the mother church of the southern part of the forest and stands in isolation to the north of the main village. The vicarage, now called after Gilpin, stood to the south, on Vicar's Hill. In School Lane, between Vicar's Hill and Pilley, stands 'Spinners', one of several nurseries in the area.

Ringwood

South of Moyles Court, the A31 slices the Ringwood area in two. To the north are extensive, largely coniferous plantations of

Street lamp, Ringwood

Ringwood Forest, and the meadows and old gravel workings of the valley of the Hampshire Avon, now used for windsurfing and water-skiing. To the south, where the river forms the boundary between Hampshire and Dorset, are found most of the services of the old market town, including its modern swimming-baths and leisure centre.

Ringwood is a pleasant place to while away an hour or two, especially on market days, when the centre is packed with stalls. It is not a town with any remarkable sights, though there are a number of interesting 18th-century buildings, such as the non-conformist house that gave its name to Meeting House Lane, and the extremely elegant Greyfriars in Christchurch Road, which is now owned by the local community association. Also of interest is Monmouth House in West Street, where in 1685 the unfortunate loser of the battle of Sedgemoor spent the night after being found in a ditch, just across the county border.

Burley, to the southeast of Ringwood, is a popular place with souvenir hunters, but it reminds me more of the West Country than the forest. The activities of the eccentric Thomas Eyre, once a lord of the manor, are evident in the village. At Queens Head Hill is the Bread Stone which he set up in 1815, to provide a queuing-point for charity. It is inscribed: 'Rest and be thankful.' And a few years later, to the west of the village he erected a stone at Black Bush, Castle Hill Lane, to mark the site of a prehistoric camp. This time the homily is: 'Be civil, quiet and useful.'

William Gilpin (1724–1804) and the Picturesque
Consideration of the principles which dictate that some views are 'pretty' and others are not was a subject which William Gilpin made his own in the late 18th century. He travelled extensively in the Lake District and other mountainous areas of Britain and wrote influential critiques of scenery for the painter and the tourist. His books were a great success, for roads had improved dramatically and the Grand Tour of Europe was hampered by social and political instability.

Gilpin did much of his travelling during a long period when he kept a school at Cheam in Surrey. But he did not begin to publish his observations until he came to Hampshire, where in 1777 he took the living of Boldre in the New Forest. After many years' deliberation he published his *Remarks on Forest Scenery*. He was so enamoured of the view from the windows of the rectory at Vicars Hill, Boldre, that he said it was 'enough to make a man jump out of them'.

Although Gilpin's approach now seems overly self-conscious, he had his influence on the landscape designers of his day and thus did much to influence the appearance of classic English parkland. His earnest studies of scenery were parodied by the satirist William Combe, whose character 'Dr Syntax' on his horse 'Grizzle' underwent a series of misfortunes.

5 Andover and the Test Valley

The Test is a relatively small river with a big reputation, at least in sporting circles. Its trout and salmon are legendary. Fishing the dry fly on its waters is generally reckoned to be a sport beyond compare. Such is its lure that in July 1944, when General Eisenhower might have been expected to spend every moment on the aftermath of D-Day, he came to Stockbridge and caught a 2-lb trout. It was rather like Drake playing bowls!

The Test is a chalk stream: it carries the waters that fall on the northern downs to the sea at Southampton. It rises near Overton and is joined by several tributaries, notably the Bourne, the Anton and the Wallop Brook. Despite having a multi-million pound factory on its uppermost reaches, namely the paper-mills of Portals, its alkaline waters have that unfailing crystal clarity for which chalk streams are renowned. In high summer the valley of the Test is one of the classic areas of the English countryside. It is also one of the few areas to have been designated an ESA (environmentally sensitive area). The Test Way is a long-distance footpath which traverses almost the whole length of the river. The great charm of the Test is carried into its tributaries. The Wallops, the Clatfords and the villages of the Bourne Valley are a delight to explore.

The main town of the valley is Andover, which has a large modern shopping centre and many other facilites. Stockbridge and Whitchurch are much smaller. Romsey, with its splendid Norman abbey, is a sizable town of outstanding historic interest.

The main tourist attractions of the area include Mottisfont Abbey, Danebury Ring, Whitchurch Silk Mill and the Hawk Conservancy at Weyhill. The Museum of Army

Fishing the Test

Flying at Middle Wallop and Andover's Museum of the Iron Age are of national importance.

ANDOVER

The old market town of Andover sits on the River Anton, a tributary of the Test, and is bypassed by the A303 main London–Exeter road. It was converted by the London overspill policies of the 1960s into one of the fastest-growing towns in the country: it is surrounded by factories and housing estates and encircled by inner and outer ring roads. Amongst the household names that are now based in the town are the tea people Twinings.

Andover is also the seat of the Test Valley Borough Council, a creation of the local government reorganisation of 1974. Just to the north of the modern shopping centre are the swimming pool and sports centre and the Cricklade Theatre. Markets are held on Thursdays and Saturdays in the High Street, which is the focal point of the town, with its fine town hall of 1825. But the hub of activity is its modern shopping precinct to the north, where most of the familiar 'High Street' chain stores can be found. Much of old Andover remains: its fine coaching inns are well worth finding when the supermarket trolley has been emptied. A convenient place to relax is the small area of parkland to the west of High Street, around the river and Town Mills.

Andover contains the Museum of the Iron Age, which stands a short distance to the north-east of the shopping centre and east of the prominent church tower. The displays are based on finds from archaeological digs at *Danebury Ring*, near Stockbridge. The museum also holds local displays, including a fish aquarium that mimics the habitat of the Test and other chalk streams and a gallery devoted to a former local ironworks, Taskers of Andover, whose traction engines were

Andover

Population: 30,932

Market Days: Thu, Sat

Cashpoints: *Barclays* 5 High St; *Lloyds* 22 High St; *Midland* 28 High St; *NatWest* Town Centre, 22 Chantry Way

Tourist Information: Town Mill Car Park, Bridge St

Attractions: Andover Museum, Finkley Down Farm and Country Park*

Arts: Cricklade Theatre

Leisure: Andover Indoor Sports Centre, Charlton Outdoor Leisure Centre

Cinema: Savoy Cinema

By Road: London 68 miles (A303, M3), Winchester 16 miles (A303, A34), Basingstoke 22 miles (A303, M3)

By Rail: 1hr 10mins from London (Waterloo to Exeter line). Direct services to Basingstoke and Salisbury

The Andover workhouse
The Poor Law Reform Act of 1834 created the notorious system of workhouses, where the poor, the sick and the unfortunate were forced to live if they required any form of state relief. Andover's workhouse held about 200 inmates under the control of a master and the direction of a Board of Guardians. Days were spent crushing bones for manure and the inmates were so ill-fed that they often ate rotting bone marrow.

The Andover workhouse was no worse than many others, but its iniquity has been remembered because it became the subject of a series of articles published in *The Times*. This led eventually to an investigation by a Select Committee, after which the master resigned. But the chairman of the board, the Rev Christopher Dodson, rector of Grateley and Penton Mewsey, continued in office until his death in 1876. He made an attempt to resign a few years after the scandal, but no-one wanted the job!

People were still living in workhouses until their demise after the National Assistance Act of 1948.

The poorhouses that many parishes had owned before the 1834 Act were also less than popular. That at Selborne came to the fore in the 1830 agricultural riots, when a mob broke down the doors and burned the furniture. The fracas was led by the Selborne trumpeter, John Newland, commemorated under the Selborne yew.

once used throughout the country. A fine Tasker bridge takes the footpath called Ladies Walk over the Old Micheldever Road, which runs from the east end of London Street.

Like many industrialists, the Taskers were non-conformists: there are family memorials outside the entrance to the United Reformed Church in Andover (high up on a wall to the south), which itself dates from 1700. By comparison, the existing parish church was built only in 1840–6, albeit on the site of a medieval church. Its highlight is the monument to Richard Kemis, who died in 1611. It depicts his large family, including a black-capped step-daughter who showed him 'malicious unkindness'.

Two miles from the town is Finkley Down Farm and Country Park, whose collections of animals and birds are particularly popular with young children. There is also a 'Barn of Bygones' and a collection of gypsy caravans. The farm is just off the north-east corner of the ring road, between Picket Piece and the Walworth Industrial Estate.

One of Andover's greatest claims to fame is its former workhouse, which was built in 1836. Reports of notorious goings-on by *The Times* in the last century did much to focus national attention on the lot of the poor. The old building still stands on the west side of the town, in Junction Road, which as its name suggests is a short walk from the railway station.

Junction Road continues north to **Charlton**, where a large area around the headwaters of the River Anton makes a pleasant open-air, lakeside sports centre, with canoeing, mini-golf, fishing and a children's playground. Further north stands Charlton's church of about 1830. This incorporates much of the fabric of the medieval church of nearby Foxcotte, which was once a thriving settlement.

The tower of the old church still remains a mile to the west of Charlton, where it forms part of an intriguing private house.

To the north of Andover are the high downs of the Hampshire–Berkshire borders. They were called the Hampshire Highlands by George Dewar (1862–1934), the naturalist/writer who roamed far and wide around his family home at Doles Wood, then in the parish of Knight's Enham. The heart of this old village and its delightful little church still survive. But the centre of activity hereabouts is at **Enham-Alamein** to the north, a settlement where disabled people work and live. It owes its origins to the aftermath of World War I, when a 'village centre' for severely injured servicemen was set up at Enham. The Alamein part of its name was added after the last war, when an Egyptian gift of £225,000 was given to commemorate the famous desert victory of Field-Marshal Montgomery. Today Enham Industries employs a wide range of disabled people at a variety of jobs, from precision engineering to furniture-making. Its Garden Centre is open daily and a small El Alamein museum stands alongside its church a mile to the north of Knight's Enham.

To the south-east of Andover is the church of **Abbot's Ann**, which is famous for its virgins' crowns. These hang on either side of the nave and are made of hazelwood and paper rosettes. Each bears five parchment gauntlets on strings. They are carried at the funerals of unmarried men or women in a ceremony which has its origins in the Middle Ages. If after three weeks the virginity of the person is unchallenged the crown is placed in position. The oldest surviving crown was made in 1740, the most recent in 1973.

Abbot's Ann stands beside the Pillhill Brook, the lower section of which runs through **Anna Valley**. It was here at the local smithy

The Iron Age: barbarians and Celts

Hampshire is an ideal place to catch up with the Iron Age. Not only does it have an open-air museum of Celtic farming at Butser, but Danebury Ring and the Museum of the Iron Age at Andover present some of the latest research on the subject. Also, the museum at Silchester shows how such sites made the transition from Celtic settlement to Roman town, whilst Fishbourne Palace, near Chichester, demonstrates the great wealth of Celtic 'client princes'.

In broad terms, throughout Europe the settled Celtic society of the first millennium BC was over-run by the Romans from about 150BC. Caesar's conquest of Gaul forced some Celtic tribes to flee. One of these, the Atrebates, settled at Silchester in about 50BC. But there was, of course, a large indigenous population in the British Isles.

The most obvious remains of the Iron Age are the great hill-forts, the first of which to be properly excavated was on St Catherine's Hill, Winchester. The latest is Danebury Ring, near Stockbridge, where 20 seasons of excavation have just been completed. Hill-forts were probably relatively sophisticated settlements which were abandoned, perhaps violently, in the last century BC. Thereafter, in the final years of the Iron Age, people moved to lower ground.

that Robert Tasker (1785–1873), a Wiltshire man, found work in 1806. Subsequently he and his brother designed and built 'improved ploughs' and other agricultural machinery on a site which they reclaimed from the marshlands alongside the Pillhill Brook. The chalk pits they dug can still be seen. This was the start of a long history of activity on the site, notably the construction of traction engines from 1869 and 'Little Giant' steam tractors after the repeal in 1896 of the 'Red Flag' act. There are still traces of what became Waterloo Ironworks, including a workman's club of 1867 and a terrace of foundrymen's houses. The flint-dressed lodge opposite Bury Hill Close served the ironmaster's house.

Bury Hill, which stands to the south of Anna Valley, is the site of a prehistoric hillfort. A pleasant path encircles the old ramparts.

A minor road runs along the north bank of the Pillhill to **Weyhill**, which was once the site of an agricultural fair of national importance. Sheep was its mainstay and it grew up here because it was convenient for London and easily reached by well-established east–west routes. Its prices set the level for the whole country. It may even have been established before the Saxon period. In the 14th century William Langland mentioned it in *Piers Plowman* and, as 'Weydon Priors', it was where Michael Henchard sold his wife in Hardy's *Mayor of Casterbridge*. The Weyhill Fair pub, which stands beside the busy A303, has an upstairs room devoted to the fair, which attracted an enormous 'fringe' of travellers and gypsies.

A mile to the west lies the Hawk Conservancy, where a large number of birds of prey (falcons, hawks and owls) can be seen in captivity. Weather permitting, there are regular displays of the exciting art of falconry. Keeping birds in cages can be offensive, but this is much more than a tourist venue. The

Conservancy is actively involved in the care of injured wild birds and in 'breed and release' programmes. There are many photo opportunities and the chance to see, and even hold, some splendid creatures.

Speed of a different kind is found at the **Thruxton Circuit** nearby, which is the home of the British Automobile Racing Club (BARC). The 2.356-mile circuit runs round a former airfield. It came to the fore in 1968, when the BARC was obliged to give up its HQ at Goodwood. Nine motor-car and three motor-cycle meetings are held each year. The key event is the Formula Three race held on Easter Monday.

Thruxton village and the countryside around are delightful. Appleshaw and Kimpton on the edge of Salisbury Plain are particularly pretty villages, though the tower of Kimpton church is an eyesore. If you take a walk hereabouts, beware the rifle ranges to the west of Kimpton Down, where the men of Tidworth Garrison may be in action.

To the south, back across the A303, are the villages of Amport and Quarley. **Amport House**, which can be seen from the road between Monxton and Quarley (formerly the route of an important Roman road), was built in 1857 for the 14th Marquess of Winchester, whose coat of arms appears on the sign of the local pub. The house is now the Chaplains School of the RAF, a function which still seems to bring it within the Official Secrets Act!

Quarley Hill contains the ramparts of a well-preserved Iron Age hillfort – definitely worth a look. A well-marked earthwork, probably a boundary, runs from the south-west of the hill for almost 2 miles to the north-west. A footpath runs up to the site from Quarley Manor Farm, which is on the turn-off to Quarley from the Amport–Grateley road. Quarley's isolated church is of great interest: it contains three Anglo-Saxon windows. Its east

The Army Flying Corps
The advantages of being able to spy on the enemy from a great height have long been recognised by military commanders, as detailed in the Museum of Army Flying at Middle Wallop. Balloons were used towards the end of the last century in several campaigns, notably in South Africa during the Boer War of 1899–1902.

In 1906, the flying interests of the British Army moved to Laffans Plain, Farnborough. Here, under the inspiration of the maverick American Sam Cody, experiments were carried out with man-lifting kites, airships and eventually aircraft. The invention of the aeroplane led in 1912 to the formation of the Royal Flying Corps, which played an important role in World War I. Thereafter, military flying was dominated by the RAF, though the observation needs of the army continued to be served. The invention of the helicopter brought back the initiative to the army. In 1957 the Army Air Corps was formed with its HQ at Middle Wallop, where the Experimental Helicopter Unit had been formed in 1955. A succession of helicopter types, including those equipped with anti-tank missiles, have now demonstrated the effectiveness of these machines in modern warfare. In particular, they proved to be invaluable in the 1982 Falklands campaign.

window of 1723 is one of the earliest known in the Palladian style, and its three bells hang at ground level, beneath an oak-shingled canopy.

Nearby **Grateley** is one of the few villages still to have its own railway station, ideal for bikers who fancy a spin in the countryside. To the south lie the Wallops, a pretty string of villages which take their names from the brook which rises in Over Wallop and drains into the Test at Bossington. The charm of this part of Hampshire comes from the preponderance of thatch: no other roofing material enables cottages to blend together so well. Thatched walls are a common sight in the Test Valley.

Since 1940 **Middle Wallop** has been the home of the army flying. Here army pilots are trained on light aircraft and helicopters on an airfield which stretches north from the village, along the A343 Salisbury–Andover road. There is public access to the Museum of Army Flying, a modern well-arranged attraction that must be visited by anyone with the slightest interest in flying. The story of the progressive involvement of the army in balloons, man-lifting kites and aircraft is one that is often overshadowed by the Orville/Wright saga. Gliders too were once army business and played a vital role in D-Day and other actions. Recent actions in the South Atlantic and Northern Ireland are chronicled.

The jewel of the Wallop Brook is the relatively large village of **Nether Wallop**, which can easily be missed, as most of it lies to the west of the B3084. Very pleasant for a stroll. Outside the west end of the church stands an enormous pyramidal tomb, once topped by a lighted torch. This was built for the eccentric Dr Francis Douce, who was buried there in 1760.

The church itself contains the most interesting set of wall paintings to have survived in the county. Unlike most such survivals, the original pictures can be picked out quite easily. There are fine 15th-century paintings of 'St George and the Dragon' and 'The Sabbath Breakers' (south wall of nave) and 'St Nicholas' (window opening in south aisle). But the most interesting painting is the fragment over the chancel arch, which is in the style of the Winchester School. The fluttering hemline of the angels has enabled it to be dated to about 1030, an exciting discovery that has added Nether Wallop to that select list of pre-1066 churches.

ROMSEY

'So drunk they must have been to Romsey' is a local saying which could once have applied to any Hampshire town on market day. But Romsey and beer do have a special link, for this was the heart of 'the Strong Country', a geographical invention of the PR department of the local brewery. Until recently its vats were bubbling away a few hundred yards from the great abbey for which the town is generally known.

You have to cross water to reach the centre of Romsey, which stands on two islands, surrounded by the waters of the Test. The abbey is undoubtedly Romsey's greatest treasure, but it is a pleasant town in its own right: easy to walk round, with a strong local character and not too self-conscious. Its triangular Market Place is still a definite centre (though the market is defunct). The lofty statue of Prime Minister Palmerston at its centre is both a landmark and tribute to a famous local man.

The Market Place once stood 'before the abbey', though the shops to the west (including Shaw's fine 18th-century façade) have grown up to obscure this relationship. The abbey is most pleasantly reached via the abbey gatehouse (which is actually part of the Congregational church of 1888) on the west side of the Market Place. This leads to a street confusingly called the Abbey, which curls

Romsey

Population: 15,039

Early Closing: Wed

Market Day: Sat

Cashpoints: *Midland* 10 Market Pl; *NatWest* 27 Market Pl

Tourist Information: Bus Station Car Park, Broadwater Rd (summer only)

Attractions: Broadlands*, Romsey Abbey

Arts: Plaza Theatre

By Road: London 75 miles (A31, A33, M3), Winchester 11 miles (A31, A3090), Southampton 8 miles (A3057)

By Rail: 1 hr 30 mins from London (branch of main Waterloo to Weymouth line). Direct services to Southampton and Salisbury

Nether Wallop church

round the site of the domestic buildings of the nunnery that once served the abbey itself.

The existing abbey church was started in the early 11th century and extended at the west end about 100 years later. The transition from the rounded arches of the Norman masons to the pointed ones of the Early English designers is seen between the third and fourth bays. The Norman work is outstanding and has a dignified grandeur which is extremely impressive. The miraculous survival of the abbey after the Dissolution as the parish church is attributed to the fact that part of the church (an extension to the north aisle, now demolished) had always been used for worship by the townspeople.

The remains of the north porticus or transept of an earlier Anglo-Saxon church can be found to the east of the north door. This is associated with the refounding of the abbey in AD967 by King Edgar (the original foundation in AD907 was by King Edward the Elder, for his daughter). Like other medieval nunneries it became an important refuge for royal ladies and other women of rank. Henry I plucked his first bride, Matilda, from the cloisters of Romsey Abbey. Prudently, the abbess judged that she had not taken the veil!

Romsey Abbey

There are other traces of the Saxon church inside, beneath a trapdoor on the north side of the choir screen that faces the north transept. Nearby is a list of abbesses of Romsey, including Alicia de Wyntershull, who died from poison in 1314, apparently without suspicion of foul play.

Proceeding around the church clockwise, there is a fine 12th-century wall painting in the second bay at the east end. To the south of it is a rare Saxon rood of about AD1000. Below the altar steps, on the south side, is the Broadlands pew, still used by Lord Romsey and his family and a rare example of a private seat in a public church. On the east side of the south transept is the grave of Lord Romsey's grandfather, Earl Mountbatten of Burma, who was assassinated by Irish extremists in 1979, only months after Broadlands House had been opened to the public. The grave lies beneath a fine memorial to the St Barbe family, who were earlier owners of the house.

In front of the abbess's doorway at the east end of the south aisle hangs a fine embroidery made in Southampton in 1966. Especially interesting of the many monuments within the abbey is a recumbent effigy of Sir William Petty FRS (1623–87), which lies at the west end. He was born in Romsey and became a distinguished scientist and a pioneering econometrician.

One other sight outside the abbey which should not be missed is the celebrated Romsey Rood, a rare calvary of the 11th century which is embedded in the west wall of the south transept.

Facing the east end of the church on the opposite side of Church Street is a short path that leads to King John's House, a 13th-century hunting box that is open to the public. It remained unrecognised until the present century. The coats of arms of aristocrats who stayed here when Edward I was in town, together with a crude caricature of the king himself, can still be seen scratched in the old plasterwork.

Since the dissolution of the abbey, Romsey has lived under the influence of successive owners of **Broadlands House**, which stands to the south of the town. Here lived Lord Palmerston and Lord Mountbatten. The house itself is a fine example of a lavishly furnished mid-Georgian mansion in the Palladian style. It is still very much a home: both the Queen and Prince Philip and the Prince and Princess of Wales came to Broadlands at the start of their honeymoons. The house contains Palmerston's library and a room devoted to relics of the great

Sir William Petty FRS (1623–87)

Doctor, scientist, musician, econometrician, naval architect, surveyor and man of business – these are just some of the accomplishments of a man who is credited with 'bringing back to life' a woman hanged for murder. The incident occurred whilst he was at Oxford, teaching anatomy and physic. The poor woman was intended as a specimen, but revived!

William Petty was born to a clothier's wife at Romsey, where he is buried. He attended the local grammar school and then studied on the Continent. At Oxford he became involved in the early meetings of the Royal Society and was a founding member of its council. During Cromwell's rule he held lucrative appointments in Ireland, where he was granted large estates that had been forfeited in the Irish rebellion of 1641. He set up a variety of enterprises, including an ironworks, a pilchard fishery, a timber business and lead mines, all in Kerry.

William Petty managed to pursue a public career and maintain his academic interests. He wrote influential economic treatises in which he argued that wealth and land, rather than gold and silver, are the bases of wealth. His action was as good as his word: he died with a vast fortune, which his grandson later used to buy an estate at Bowood, Wiltshire, where his descendants still live.

**Earl Mountbatten of Burma
(1900–79)**
Lord Louis Mountbatten
came to live at Broadlands
House by virtue of his
marriage in 1922 to the
heiress Edwina Ashley. His
parents were Lord Louis of
Battenberg and Princess
Victoria of Hesse, which
made him a great-grandson
of Queen Victoria. During
World War I, the family
adopted the name of
Mountbatten.

During a brilliant naval
career he moved from being
a specialist in wireless
telegraphy to becoming
Chief of the Defence Staff
and Chairman of the Chief
of Staffs Committee. He is
probably best known for his
command of Allied forces in
Burma, where he forced
back the Japanese and
helped liberate south-east
Asia. This followed a
distinguished record of
naval command and a
period when, as Chief of
Combined Operations, he
had been involved in plans
for D-Day and other
campaigns.

After the war, Lord
Mountbatten became the
last Viceroy of India and in
1947 presided over the
division of the Indian sub-
continent into India and
Pakistan.

Amongst his many
peacetime appointments
was that of Governor of the
Isle of Wight, an ancient
post which in 1974
disappeared when the
island became a county. He
had no sons and was
granted the privilege of
allowing his title to pass to
his eldest daughter, who
became the 2nd Countess of
Mountbatten.

Prime Minister, including the tiny desk at
which he worked standing up. The former
stables of the house contain an exhibition of
the life of Lord Mountbatten (1900–79) – his
wartime roles in south-east Asia and the 1944
invasion of Europe, his appointment as the last
Viceroy of India and much else. Also on
display are replicas of the crown jewels of the
world.

Another fine house near Romsey is
Mottisfont Abbey, which lies three miles to the
north and is owned by the National Trust. Like
Broadlands, it stands in fine countryside on
sloping lawns beside the River Test. It was
founded in 1201 as an Augustinian priory. The
site was probably chosen for its unfailing
spring of clear fresh water which still spills out
200 gallons of water per minute.

After the suppression of the priory in 1536
it passed to the Lord Chamberlain, William
Lord Sandys, who already owned the Vyne at
Sherborne St John, near Basingstoke. He
acquired his new home in exchange for land in
the villages of Chelsea and Paddington. Little
of the mansion he built on to the old priory
church survives, and most of what can be seen
today is of a smaller mid-18th-century house
built by Sir Richard Mill, who preferred to refer
to Mottisfont as an abbey rather than a mere
priory.

The highlight of the interior of the house is
a room decorated by the theatrical artist Rex
Whistler just before the last war, during which
he was killed in action. Its lavish opulence is
softened by the personal touches of the artist: a
pot and brush apparently left beside the bay
window, a smoking urn that looks like the real
thing, a personal message that reads: 'I was
painting this ermine curtain when Britain
declared war on the Nazi tyrants.'

Mottisfont itself is a pretty village with a
tea-shop and a charming church (once under
the archbishop of York). Indeed, almost any

part of the Test Valley from here to its source is fine country, ideal for a picnic.

The grounds of the abbey contain the National Trust national collection of historic roses, which is invaluable for putting names to flowers and appreciating the subtle differences between varieties, particularly the older ones. Another delight for gardeners lies to the west of Romsey, between the villages of Ampfield and Braishfield. This is the **Hillier Arboretum**, a vast collection of trees and woody plants which represents the lifelong work of the horticulturalist Sir Harold Hillier (1905–85). Its first curator was the media gardener Roy Lancaster, who was appointed in 1970. It is now owned by the county council.

This collection covers 100 acres of sand and clay soils and includes varieties from all five continents. There is always something worth seeing, from the witch hazels of mid-winter to the rhododendrons of early summer and the leafy hues of autumn. The serious gardener will need a notebook and a camera to prevent 'label fatigue', whilst those who are less keen can treat it as a woodland ramble.

Also on this side of Romsey is the Michelmersh Brick Works, not exactly a tourist attraction but well-known for its traditional hand-made bricks and other products. It must surely be the only brickworks to have featured on BBC's *Tomorrow's World*, who reported an innovation that has dramatically improved its input. Someone realised that it would be better to design a furnace so that it could be moved to the wet clay, rather than vice versa.

Many country parks have been set up throughout the county in recent years, but one which is rather special is to be found at Ower, five miles down the A31 Romsey–Southampton road. This is Paulton's Country Park, the creation of the Mancey family, which in 1988 attracted more than 370,000 visitors. It is just off Junction 2 of the

**Florence Nightingale
(1820–1910)**
In 1854 the British
authorities were jerked
awake by reports that *soeurs
de charité* were caring for
French soldiers in the
Crimea, whereas British
men injured in the same
conflict were suffering the
most appalling hardships.
As a result, the secretary
for war invited a young
lady called Florence
Nightingale to take out a
group of nurses to the war.
Florence had, at her own
initiative, taken a deep
interest in nursing and had
trained on the Continent.

The 'lady of the lamp',
as she was called, brought
care and dignity to
wounded men who had
previously not even been
given beds to lie on. One
memento of the times
which can be seen in East
Wellow church, where she
worshipped, is a cross
made from round shot from
the battlefield of Scutari.

One immediate effect of
the Crimean War was the
building of the Royal
Victoria Hospital at Netley.
Of more lasting significance
was the founding in 1861 of
the first nurses' training
school, at St Thomas's
Hospital, London.

M27 and offers a unique blend of attractions: it
is not a Disneyland theme park, it is not a
'farm turned park', it is not a stately home and
it is not a zoo. Yet it has elements of all of
these and provides a whole day out for the
family. For children it is a 'fairground' and for
adults a place to relax and look around the
Village Life Museum or the collections of exotic
waterfowl, vultures, owls and other birds. The
parklands of the former estate and a huge
undershot water-wheel can also be seen.
Particularly interesting is the Romany
Museum, which presents the lore of the
traveller and includes examples of some of the
classic types of caravans and wagons.

A few miles to the north of Ower is a quiet
backwater with a surprise. This is **East Wellow**,
a scattered village with a remote church that is
renowned as the place where Florence
Nightingale (1820–1910) lies buried. This
famous heroine of the Crimean War lived with
her parents at Embley Park near by, which is
now used as a private school.

The countryside to the west and north of
Romsey is delightfully quiet and peaceful. The
extensive commons and manorial wastes to the
south of West Wellow, which are owned by the
National Trust, extend to the edge of the New
Forest. To the north, such villages as Sherfield
English, West Dean and West Tytherley merge
effortlessly into Wiltshire. In fact, the boundary
between the two shires passes through the
middle of the Red Lion pub in West Dean! This
peaceful village has another surprise, for it is
common knowledge that nuclear weapons are
almost certainly stored under Dean Hill.

STOCKBRIDGE

A place built to catch passing trade, the 'street
town' of King's Somborne, was the origin of
Stockbridge. Travellers between Winchester
and Salisbury still are important for the trade
of the village (or is it a small town?). But the

Gate, East Wellow church

place is now best known to fishermen, some of whom are fortunate enough to sit above the great porch of the Grosvenor Hotel. Here is the clubroom of the Houghton Club, founded in 1822, an extremely exclusive fishing club with limited membership which controls several miles of fishing along the banks of the Test. The quarry is, of course, trout, the style is, of course, dry fly only, and there is no chance of casual day tickets.

More practical for the casual visitor is a forage in the seemingly countless antique shops that line the main (and only) street of the village. There are other speciality shops also, particularly if you like game food or crafts. And when shopping is over there are a few sights. My favourite is Stokes's garage, a nostalgic relic of a past age that it would be sacrilege to call a filling station. The present church is unlikely to be of interest to the outsider, nor the drab town hall, but the chancel of the old church, at the east end of the town, has some charm. In the surrounding graveyard is the tombstone of John Bucket, publican and prime fixer in the days when Stockbridge was a rotten borough that traded in votes.

It is the position of Stockbridge in the heart of the Test Valley that makes it special. The Test Way long-distance footpath passes by, alongside the old church, and there are minor roads along both sides of the river. To the south there is a pleasant route along the west side of the river, taking in charming villages like Houghton and Broughton. Houghton Lodge is a 'Nash-like' cottage built in about 1801 which opens its delightful gardens during the summer. Broughton church has a dovecote in its grounds which was restored to mark the National Heritage Year of 1984.

King's Somborne to the east is a pleasant village which was once held by John of Gaunt. His name is remembered in a 5-acre stillwater trout fishery (native brownies and beefy

Writers and the River Test
The Test Valley seems to have inspired at least one avid scribbler for each generation. In the early 19th century it was the rector of Chilbolton, Richard Durnford (1766–?1834), whose entertaining diaries were not published until 1911. Another man whose diaries took many years to be set in print was Colonel Peter Hawker (1786–1853) of Longparish, who was as much a wildfowler as a fisherman. *The Chronicles of the Houghton Fishing Club*, in two volumes, also contain much useful information on the river and its fishermen.

A man who held passionate views on fishing the chalk streams was the professional singer Harry Plunket Greene (1865–1936). He fished the Bourne rivulet, which joins the Test at Hurstbourne Priors, where he is buried (in the south-west corner of the churchyard). Another delightful writer who loved the river was John Waller Hills (1867–1938), who wrote the classic, *A Summer on the Test*, and also chronicled the life of the legendary Stockbridge keeper, William Lunn. The *Ever-Rolling Stream* by Bernard Aldrich tells the story of a modern keeper's work, from his own pen.

A more general view of the river and its valley comes from Geoffrey Snagge's *Letters from Longstock* and its sequel *More Letters*.

Long-distance footpaths in Hampshire

In recent years Hampshire County Council has waymarked five long-distance footpaths.

The *Solent Way* stretches from Milford-on-Sea in the west to Emsworth. It runs over the marshes of Keyhaven and Pennington, along the Beaulieu river and across Southampton Water at Hythe. It then keeps to the shore between Southampton and Gosport and crosses Portsmouth Harbour. The final leg passes along Southsea front and then up and around Langstone Harbour to Emsworth.

Emsworth is also at one end of the *Wayfarer's Walk* which strikes across some of the finest countryside in Hampshire. It runs up the Meon Valley and then makes for Cheriton and Alresford. It continues up the charming valley of the Candover Stream and then rises into the North Hampshire Downs, via Dummer and Oakley. It passes along the great escarpment of the downs to end at Comble Gibbet on Inkpen Beacon.

Here it meets the *Test Way*, which starts at Totton, near Southampton. This delightful route makes use of the disused line of the Test Valley Railway for much of its length. At King's Somborne it meets the *Clarendon Way*, which runs between Winchester and Southampton, keeping mostly to an old ridgeway route.

The most recent route is the *Hangers' Way*, between Petersfield and East Worldham.

rainbows). At King's Somborne the Test Way crosses the Clarendon Way, a long-distance footpath between Winchester and Salisbury. A local craft centre makes coffee tables from 'the victims' of Dutch Elm Disease, some of which are found to contain souvenirs of the last war, namely chunks of German shrapnel. There are fine views from a hill to the east of King's Somborne. This can be mounted via a short leg of the Clarendon Way, starting from the road to Little Somborne – which, incidentally, has a tiny Saxon church with Norman additions. Another interesting small church near by is that at Ashley. It was built within the defences of a Norman earthwork.

To the west of Stockbridge stand earthworks that are more than 2,500 years old and yet are still steep enough to raise the pulse. These are the remains of **Danebury** hill fort, a prehistoric defended 'town' that has been the subject of a 20-year dig by Oxford archaeologist Professor Barry Cunliffe. It has already been mentioned under *Andover*, where the Museum of the Iron Age displays finds from the site in context. The earthwork itself is one of the best-preserved in the country and is well worth a visit (no charge!).

Danebury Ring is reached via a minor road which runs off the A30, a mile to the west of Stockbridge. To the south once lay a famous race-course and stables, where several national winners were trained. The grandstand of 1831, reputed to be the oldest in the country, still stands beside the old course and can be clearly seen from the site of the hill-fort.

The valley to the north of Stockbridge is one of the prettiest in England. The best route is probably via the A3057, crossing after a mile to Longstock and then continuing up to Wherwell and the well-named Longparish, with its public grindwheel. The river is jealously guarded by landowners, but there are good viewpoints from the several bridges, whilst the Mayfly pub at Testcombe Bridge, near Fullerton, has a large frontage for the benefit of its clientele. The extensive water gardens of Longstock Park are open to the public on one Sunday each month. This delightful place belongs to the John Lewis Partnership, who since 1928 have also owned the entire village of Leckford, which stands on the opposite bank.

Places to stretch the legs include West Down, which stands to the east of the Mayfly pub, and Chilbolton Common, an area of botanical interest between two braids of the river to the north. The great white dish antenna that can be seen to the east of Chilbolton is an SERC radio telescope, situated on a former airfield where Spitfires were once assembled and tested.

Almost anywhere in this part of Hampshire there are pleasant corners and delightful pubs to be found. It is not a place of dramatic attractions but one of quiet delights, and all the better for it. At **Wherwell** there are traces of the famous Saxon Benedictine nunnery swept away by the Dissolution. At **Longparish** village stocks and a wayside cross still stand near the parish church, which itself has an interesting stained-glass window with the lower border depicting an airfield of World War I. To the west of this part of the Test Valley lies Harewood Forest, an area of old woodland criss-crossed by paths. In the forest north of the A303, a mile to the west of its intersection with the B3048, is a pretty walk leading to Deadman's Plack. This monument was erected by a 19th-century owner of Wherwell Priory, as the abbey became (cf Mottisfont Abbey, which was a priory!). It recalls the murders of the first husband and a stepson of Queen Elfrida, the second wife of King Edgar. These gory acts are said to have prompted her to take the veil and found Wherwell Abbey in AD986.

Stockbridge

WHITCHURCH

Whitchurch is a small town that returned two MPs to Westminster until the Reform Act of 1832. It has a mayor (a distinction restored in 1974), a town hall, a railway station (on the line between Andover and Basingstoke) and two major attractions. One is the Whitchurch Folk Festival, which has been held each year since 1979. The other is Whitchurch Silk Mill, a rare survival that is not a living museum but a working factory that welcomes visitors. It is owned by the Hampshire Buildings Preservation Trust.

Whitchurch Silk Mill is the last remaining relic in Hampshire of the traditional weaver's trade, an industry that was once to be found throughout the southern counties. It is strange that water-driven Whitchurch (now powered by electricity) survived, whilst similar factories elsewhere were unable to ride the ups and downs of the trade. Spinning and weaving have been carried out here since at least the 11th century, whilst silk has been made since 1830 (with powered looms since ca.1890) and once employed 100 people, many of them children. The mill prospered in the present century by concentrating on speciality materials such as electrical insulation and legal and academic silks. It now also makes quality consumer fashion silks, which are on sale in the Mill Shop, where shirts and blouses of Hampshire silk can be ordered.

Whitchurch Silk Mill

Another Whitchurch relic worth seeing is the rare Saxon tombstone which is in the parish church, next to the lectern. It commemorates Frithburga, who may have been an abbess at Wherwell.

A plaque to the north of the town hall, on the side wall of a chemist's shop, records that Whitchurch is the birthplace of Lord Denning (Master of the Rolls 1962-82), who returned to live in his home town in 1963.

The Test above Whitchurch is a curious mix

of idyllic chalk-stream countryside and discreet industry. Just as specialist silks kept Whitchurch Mill in business, so the making of specialist papers for bank notes has given work to many people upstream. Test waters are ideal for making the crisp, tough paper needed by bankers. Portals is the name that dominates this part of the river. Originally a family business, it has grown into a £200 million enterprise, still with a major interest in papermaking, but now with a larger trade in water treatment. Centred on the mill at **Laverstoke**, the group owns companies elsewhere in Britain and overseas.

Portals has a romantic past that started when the French Huguenot emigré Henry Portal fled to England in the early years of the 18th century. He landed at Southampton and learned the trade of paper-making in the town, at South Stoneham Mill on the River Itchen. By 1712 he had decided to set up in business himself and took Bere Mill, near Whitchurch, which is still owned by Portals. This beautiful mill can be reached via a narrow lane that leads down to the river on the eastern outskirts of the town, or by a footpath that starts to the east of the Silk Mill (or at the end of Town Mill Lane). The path runs east along the river, past Town Mill to Bere Mill and on to Freefolk, with its tiny whitewashed chapel (key available locally). Town Mill is a beautiful private home restored by the naturalists Ron and Rosemary Eastman, who made nature films. In 1969 they published a classic study of kingfishers on the Test. The path leads on to Laverstoke Mill, which gave Henry Portal room for expansion after only six years in business. The most important job he ever secured was in 1724, when he was given the exclusive contract (still extant) to supply paper to the Bank of England. This led to numerous other contracts with provincial banks and later with overseas governments. As security paper required close

Lord Denning
Alfred Thompson Denning was born in 1899 at Whitchurch. His father was a draper and had poems published in the *Andover Advertiser*. In the words of his famous son, he was: 'Not a man of business. Not hard enough.' But he did bring up an extraordinary family of five sons and a daughter. Two sons died during World War I, another became a general and another an admiral. And 'Tom' Denning rose to become Master of the Rolls (1962–82). The fact is celebrated on a plaque erected by the American Bar Association on the outside wall of Boorman's the chemists, beside Whitchurch town hall.

Lord Denning was educated at Andover Grammar School and Oxford, where he initially read maths. He gained a First and for a short period taught at Winchester College, but casual visits to the public gallery of the Winchester courts gave him a taste for law. So he went back to Oxford, where he gained another First, this time in law. He was called to the bar in 1923 and practised on the Western Circuit. In 1938 he was appointed KC and thereafter his career progressed rapidly.

His professional life was marked by a willingness to adapt the law to the social climate of modern times. He gave judgements on a wide variety of matters, including Freddie Laker's 'Skytrain', pornography and gaming clubs in London, and much else.

Banks and banking
The Bank of England came into being in 1694 to finance wars in Europe. Contrary to previous practice, wealthy people stumped up money without any prospect of having it paid back in their lifetime, but in the anticipation of perpetual interest, secured by the state itself. The bank-notes issued to these investors by the 'Old Lady of Threadneedle Street' were the start of the large-scale use of 'paper money', a subject which made William Cobbett's blood boil. Thus, when in 1724 Henry Portal obtained an exclusive contract to supply paper to the Bank of England, he was well on his way to a fortune. The contract was helped by an introduction from Sir William Heathcote, who had just built Hursley House, near Winchester, and whose uncle was governor of the Bank of England.

In the last century there were many small local banks, some of which got into difficulties. At Ringwood in 1821, for example, a week after the death of the respected brewer and banker Stephen Tunks, his Ringwood and Hampshire Bank suspended payments. The parish church alone had £600 on deposit. There was a happier ending at Petersfield, when in 1841 the Petersfield and Hampshire Bank faced bankruptcy. A larger bank took over the business. Its officials came to Petersfield with 'a travelling bag which defied the power of a single man to lift'!

supervision, 'Ye Bank Officer' was a frequent visitor to Laverstoke. The house in which he stayed still stands opposite the mill, on the eastern side of the road to Micheldever. A plaque records that it was built in 1785 by Joseph Portal (1720–93), who had inherited from his father in 1747. The last member of the family to be involved in the business was Sir Francis Portal, who retired in 1968.

The influence of the Portals is found everywhere in this part of the Test Valley. Paper-making on the river is now centred near the source of the river, in a factory at Overton which dates from 1922. A 'shadow' printing works was set up here by the Bank of England during the last war. Conservationists should be heartened by the fact that an industry can dominate the upper stretches of a river without destroying its value as a major trout stream. By the time the Test reaches Whitchurch it has already been used to make money (well, almost) several times!

Overton was one of the 'new towns' laid out by the bishop of Winchester in the early 13th century. Its main street is Winchester Street, which runs at right angles to the through road (cf New Alresford). The original medieval village lay to the north, where the church and 16th-century Court House still stand.

Whitchurch is a convenient place from which to explore the valley of the Bourne, a small river that disappears each summer and is reborn each winter. It runs into the Test at **Hurstbourne Priors**, which is centred on the north side of the Whitchurch–Andover road. Here are a cricket ground and church (reached by a fine double avenue of trees) and Hurstbourne Park, a private estate with oak trees which are said to be 800 years old. The most recent owner, Sir Patrick Donner (1904–88), sometime Basingstoke MP, planted more than 10,000 trees in the park during the last 50 years of his life. During the last war the house was used by the Bank of England. A great 'Celtic' cross to the north-west of the church and numerous other memorials announce that this was once the home of the Wallops, earls of Portsmouth. But the most remarkable memorial in the church is the 16th-century altar-tomb of a constable of the Tower of London, Sir Robert Oxenbridge and his wife.

Two miles to the north of Hurstbourne Priors, on the Waterloo–Exeter line, is a dramatic railway viaduct. It towers over the huge beds of Hampshire Watercress Limited who are pioneers in the cultivation of this tasty aquatic crop. Two miles further above the viaduct is the delightful village of **St Mary Bourne**, with its ancient 'summerhaugh' or village square. Its church contains the largest of the well-known Tournai marble fonts. A fine 4-mile leg of the Test Way runs from the recreation ground in the village, via Stokehill Farm and Doles Wood, to Hurstbourne Tarrant, which the radical journalist William Cobbett called 'Up Husband'. He frequently stayed here with a farmer friend.

Another visitor to this part of Hampshire was the novelist Jane Austen. She came to the chocolate-box hamlet of **Ibthorpe**, which is across the A343 Newbury–Andover road from Hurstbourne Tarrant. Ibthorpe House, where she stayed with friends, still stands.

Basingstoke

Population: 73,492

Early Closing: Thu

Market Days: Wed, Sat

Cashpoints: *Barclays* 8 Market Pl; *Lloyds* Mayfair House; *Midland* Fulham House 5 Wesley Walk, 8 London St; *Natwest* Old Market Square, 3 London St, 14 Kensington House

Tourist Information: Willis Museum, Market Square.

Attractions: Willis Museum and Art Gallery

Arts: Central Studio, Haymarket Theatre, Horseshoe Theatre Co, Sarum Hill Drama Centre

Leisure: Basingstoke Ice Rink, Basingstoke Sports Centre, Westfield Lido

Cinema: Cannon Cinema

By Road: London 49 miles (M3), Winchester 19 miles (A33)

By Rail: 45mins from London (Waterloo to Exeter and Weymouth lines). Direct Services to Andover, Farnborough, Reading and Winchester

6 Basingstoke and North-East Hampshire

There has been so much change in this part of Hampshire that the administrative districts of Hart and Rushmoor, both created in the local government reshuffle of 1974, are still not on many people's 'internal maps'. Similarly, the great extent of Basingstoke District, which is of the same vintage, is rarely appreciated. There have been other more important changes, such as the redevelopment of Basingstoke town, the building of the M3 and hectic development.

Despite rapid change, much of north-east Hampshire still offers the visitor an attractive package of pretty villages and unfrequented footpaths in unspoilt countryside. There is the added bonus of modern shops and good sports facilities in the towns of Basingstoke, Alton, Farnborough and Aldershot, with rapid access from London and south Hampshire via the M3. The area can be divided into several distinct parts. To the north-west are the delightfully empty downlands of the Hampshire–Berkshire borders. North of Basingstoke are the claylands typical of the Thames Basin, a place of ponds, ancient moated manor houses and brick-and-timber cottages. The light sandy soils of the Surrey borders are characterised by vast expanses of commons and pretty ponds and lakes. Alton and district is an area of rich meadows, hop-fields, mills and thatched cottages. The north-east corner of the county is crossed by the Basingstoke Canal, which has been restored in recent years for public use.

Amongst the treasures in this area are the great houses of the Vyne and Highclere Castle, Odiham's main street, the paintings of Stanley Spencer at Burghclere, Pamber Priory, the Alton Buckle in the Curtis Museum, Jane Austen's house at Chawton, and Watership Down and the north Hampshire hills.

BASINGSTOKE

Where was the birthplace of the founder of Merton College, Oxford? Where were Burberry coats first made? Where did Alfred Milward start his chain of shoe shops? Answer: Basingstoke!

To these arcane claims to fame can now be added the thoroughly modern story of how Basingstoke was turned from a small town of about 17,000 people in 1960 to one of more than 90,000 today. 'London overspill' was the cry of the 1960s. After hectic political manoeuvrings behind the scenes, the Hampshire County Council decided that the best place to accommodate the determined wishes of London government was Basingstoke. Interestingly, they wanted the development to be well within the county, lest later boundary changes should give the benefits of their hard work to Berkshire.

Such drastic change destroyed the existing community and made a new one. No longer is Basingstoke the small market town it once was (though it does have a market, in Old and New Market Squares), but instead it has become a major urban centre with facilities to match, including an ice rink, swimming pools (one beneath the pavements of the shopping centre), sports centre, athletics track and theatre. There are so many local societies that it takes two pages of the newspaper to accommodate them. Such is change.

Basingstoke is now the home of the Civil Service Commission, the AA, Macmillans and many other well-known organisations. Vast industrial estates and new buildings have risen up, including the glitzy downtown Provident Life building (near the Victory roundabout) and the Churchill Plaza and Sun Life buildings (near the Eastrop roundabout). A taste of the 1980s.

The story of Basingstoke from its earliest days to the present is attractively told in the

Basingstoke Town Development

Between 1962 and 1977 Basingstoke was changed utterly by a Town Development Group created under the provision of an Act of 1952. In the years that followed, the town's population was increased fivefold, in order to absorb part of London's overspill population. This involved demolishing the centre of the old town and building a new centre. At the same time, houses, industrial estates and the services needed by a modern town were all built.

Inevitably, such changes met fierce local opposition and encountered many problems. The ancient common was 'in the way' and a new one had to be created, to the east of the ring road. Completion of the outer ring road, which was eventually finished in 1976, was delayed by fears that wartime dumps of cyanide might be a health hazard.

Although modern Basingstoke is dominated by these changes, there are plenty of signs that the town was ripe for industrial expansion long before the London County Council came on the scene. Just before the outbreak of the last war, for example, Eli Lilly, then a fledging British subsidiary of the American company, built its factory on the western outskirts of the town, where it still stands. Even earlier, during World War I, Thorneycroft's had a factory at Basingstoke which turned out large numbers of lorries for the military.

Basingstoke ring road
Some people call
Basingstoke 'Doughnut
City', after the inner and
outer ring roads.

The outer ring road has
eight roundabouts and
connects with seven major
roads. Access to the outer
ring road from the M3 is at
the south-east corner. The
town centre is reached,
either from the eastern or
the western sections of the
ring road, via roundabouts
that lead to Churchill Way.
This crosses the east-west
diameter of the outer ring
and passes through the
town centre.

Inner roundabouts at the
eastern and western ends
of Churchill Way (called
Eastrop and Victory
roundabouts, respectively)
give access to the northern
and southern sectors of the
inner ring road, which are
called Alencon Link and
Timberlake Road,
respectively.

The names of the
roundabouts of the outer
ring and the major routes
with which they connect,
starting from the M3 exit at
Junction 6, and proceeding
clockwise, are:

Black Dam – A30 to
Camberley
Hackwood Road – A339 to
Alton
Winchester Road – A30 to
Winchester and Salisbury
Town Centre West – B3400 to
Basingstoke Centre or
Overton
Newbury Road – A339 to
Kingsclere and Newbury
Aldermaston Road – A340 to
Aldermaston
Reading Road – A33 to
Reading
Town Centre East – to
Basingstoke Centre

Willis Museum, which occupies the former
Town Hall in the Old Market Square. Most
revealing are the accounts of the riots that
broke out in the 1880s between members of the
Salvation Army preaching temperance and the
town rabble, egged on by local brewers.

Some of the old town that was Basingstoke
can still be found. The former Post Office in
New Street is an interesting blend of old and
new, backed by a peaceful square with a
sculpture of 'Father and Child'. But the best
bits of old Basingstoke are in Church Street,
Wote Street and traffic-free London Street,
once part of the A30. The character of the
former market town is firmly stamped on St
Michael's church and the Lesser Market and
the Corn Exchange (now the Haymarket
Theatre) in Wote Street. Sir James Deane's
almhouses of 1608 at the east end of London
Street are charming. Rail travellers have a
grandstand view of the Holy Ghost Chapel, a
medieval institution refounded as a guild
chapel by Lord Sandys (d.1540) of the Vyne,
who is buried there.

Basingstoke is ringed by roads that have a
reputation for getting you lost. In fact, its
modern traffic system is extremely effective,
though some familiarity with the names of the
seemingly endless ring of roundabouts is
useful. Peace and quiet can be found in Eastrop
Park and on the common, which are on the
east side of the town. A quiet out-of-town
venue is the Viables Craft Centre, to the south
of the south-west corner of the ring-road, in
Harrow Way (on the line of the prehistoric
track). It's ideal for watching craftsmen at
work, and sipping a glass of wine. West Ham
Park, on the west of town, has a lido,
swimming pool and nine-hole golf course,
whilst occasional games of county cricket are
played in the ground in Bounty Road.

It is not obvious, but Basingstoke is near the
source of the river Loddon, which runs north

to join the Thames. It was in this general direction that the town first tried to forge a canal link with London in 1769. However, when the Basingstoke Canal was eventually realised, 25 years later, it ran to the east, via Fleet, Aldershot and Woking, to join the River Wey Navigation at West Byfleet. It required 29 locks, most of them in the Surrey side, to cover 37 miles.

Although the canal continued to carry traffic until after the last war, it was never a commerical success and would have closed were it not for the heroic efforts of the volunteers of the Surrey and Hampshire Canal Society and the respective county councils. With the exception of the length from Basingstoke to the derelict Greywell Tunnel, which is an incredible 1,230yds long, the western end of the canal has now been restored to the Surrey borders and beyond. Conceived with the mundane aim of shifting corn to London and bringing back coal, it has become a prime leisure facility. It has also become remarkable for wildlife: it has habitats for a variety of water plants, water birds can be seen close to, and bats hibernate in the Greywell Tunnel.

The western end of the unrestored bed of the canal skirts the ruins of Basing House, a Royalist stronghold of the Civil War. It eventually fell in 1645 after a two-year seige. In the final phase Oliver Cromwell took personal direction of the troops: it needed 7,000 Roundheads to quell 300 Royalists.

The house stood on a site which was of importance in Saxon times and probably lent its name to Basingstoke and London's Basinghall.

The remains of the palatial brick-built Tudor house that Cromwell almost destroyed can still be seen, together with surviving dovecotes and an attractive small museum that explains the importance of Basing House and the successive

The Basingstoke Canal
The entire length of the towpath of the canal, from North Warnborough to West Byfleet is a public footpath. The Hampshire section, which is almost entirely rural, keeps to the north side of the canal. There is a large public car park with boats for hire at Colt Hill Wharf, near Odiham, and there are other car parks at Barley Mow, near Winchfield, at Crookham Wharf, at Rushmoor Flash, near Aldershot, and elsewhere. Licensed private boats can be launched. The narrow boat *John Pinkerton*, named after the canal's engineer, makes regular cruises and can be hired. Also for hire is the *Mildred Stocks*, which can take wheelchairs. The waterway and its wildlife are the main attractions, but there are some sights, including King John's Castle at North Warnborough, and the part-folly part-lodge at Wilk's Water to the east of Odiham.

All these opportunities for enjoyment have resulted from the efforts of the volunteers of the Surrey and Hampshire Canal Society, which was formed in 1966. At this time the canal was in a poor state of repair, partly due to the destruction in 1957 of a lock at Frimley by troops returning from an exercise. Protracted negotiations with the owners of the canal had by 1976 brought the whole of its length into the ownership of the county councils of Hampshire and Surrey.

members of the Paulet dynasty (Marquises of Winchester) who lived there. Costumed guides are often on hand and re-enactments by the English Civil War Society are a regular feature. The stout in heart can crawl down a secret passage – or was it a drain? The fine gardens of the Tudor mansion are being reconstructed.

Basing village was built largely from the rubble of the old house. It is a pretty place and the local church is full of Paulet memorials. Also worth visiting on the east side of Basingstoke is the tiny Nately Scures church, one of only three surviving examples of a simple aisleless Norman church with a rounded east end. It contains an eccentric set of memorials shaped like the four suits of cards. These commemorate members of the Carleton family, Lords Dorchester, who lived in the neighbouring village of Greywell. A footpath from the centre of Greywell runs from the end of the great canal tunnel already mentioned, beside an aqueduct which carries the canal over the river Whitewater, and on to King John's Castle (also known as Odiham Castle). The impressive remains of this medieval building, which can be reached from North Warnborough, were once recognisable as those of an octagonal keep, the only one known in England. It was from here that King John rode to Runnymede to sign the Magna Carta in 1215. The troubles of his reign are reflected in the fact that in the following year the castle was beseiged by the French Dauphin.

The canal continues to the outskirts of **Odiham**, with which Domesday Book begins, which has the finest High Street in Hampshire, mainly 18th- and 19th-century façades with some much older structures behind. Seventeeth-century wall paintings were recently discovered in the George Inn.

Odiham's peaceful old market square is called the Bury. It lies to the south of the High Street. Near by are the parish stocks (not used,

Nately Scures church

as far as I know) and the church, a huge and rather grim building, but with some interesting brasses and attractive modern stained glass. To the south of the church, and tactlessly close to the graveyard, is the Pest House of 1625, an isolation hospital now a small museum.

North of the town a minor road leads across Odiham Common to **Winchfield** church, which is renowned for its rich Norman carving. Further north is **Hartley Wintney**, a place of antique shops (or so it seems), rather spoilt by the busy A30, but with a pleasant common planted with oak trees and an ancient cricket ground which is said to be the oldest in England. The surrounding countryside is crossed by many woodland walks. To the south-west is **West Green House**, an early 18th-century National Trust property. It can be visited on written application only, though its gardens are open on some afternoons.

West Green House was owned by General 'Hangman' Hawley (1679–1759), who helped massacre the Scots at Culloden. A much more celebrated soldier in Hampshire is the Duke of Wellington, whose fabulously furnished house at **Stratfield Saye** is open to the public. It is one huge memorial to that unfashionable type, the great military hero. He beat the French at Waterloo, and he also beat them in India and Spain. The house and estate were given to him by 'a grateful nation'. The duke's life is told in the former stable block of the house. There are those famous Wellington boots, his underclothes (embroidered with a W and coronet), his throat-warmer, his fearsome false teeth and much else. The prime exhibit is, however, his 'funeral car', a grotesque 18-ton mobile bier. Unfortunately, at the critical moment this 'monsterpiece' of Victorian engineering failed: a turntable jammed and kept the congregation in St Paul's waiting for 90 minutes.

No visit to Stratfield Saye is complete

The Duke of Wellington (1769–1852)
The 'Great Duke' was a man of great complexity and some mystery. At least five different dates, and no fewer than 11 locations, have been suggested for his birth.

He was so much a soldier that he could never quite settle down to an ordinary domestic existence. Until his dying day he slept on a camp bed and he never took much interest in aggrandising the house he owned at Stratfield Saye. He did, however, lavish great attention on the estate.

After returning to England from his great victory at Waterloo, Wellington had in 1818 entered politics, though he detested the manoeuvrings of party politics. Ten years later, after resigning from an earlier cabinet, he became prime minister. Paradoxically, for a man who was a traditionalist – and an Irish-born Protestant – it was under his administration that Catholics were given their long-overdue right to take up public office. But Wellington was totally opposed to the abolition of 'rotten boroughs' and other reforms of parliament, which led to the downfall of his government on 16 November 1830. On the very next day he was brought face to face with the bitter realities of the mob, when rioting started in Hampshire. As lord lieutenant of the county, he was responsible for marshalling troop to troubled areas.

Silchester

So many modern towns have grown up on the site of a Roman settlement that the notion of a Roman town that was 'unsuccessful' is unfamiliar. This was the fate of Silchester, which can perhaps be thought of as ceding a little of its territorial power to each of the nearest towns of Newbury, Basingstoke and Reading (where so many of its relics are in the museum).

Silchester was originally a settlement of the Atrebates, a Celtic tribe. Under the Romans it became *Calleva Atrebatum*, an administrative centre and market town with the facilities typical of the Roman way of life. These included an amphitheatre (at the north-east corner, seating perhaps as many as 9,000), a forum and basilica (market place and town hall), public baths and churches. The most exciting find at Silchester is a small building with a transept which some experts have claimed to be the earliest known Christian church in Britain. If it was Christian, it must have been built after the Roman authorities came to tolerate Christianity in AD313.

The walls at Silchester, which enclose an area almost as large as that of Roman Winchester, are the most obvious relics of the town. They were first built in the late 2nd century AD and replaced in the late 3rd century. There are traces of the walls over their entire 1½-mile circuit. Experts have calculated that they required 150,000 wagon loads of flint and bonding stone.

without a stroll in the grounds to find the tombstone of Wellington's horse Copenhagen, of whom he said: 'for bottom and endurance I never saw his fellow'. On the other side of the A33 from the house is the Wellington Country Park. Here there are water sports, riding, crazy golf, a 'time trail' (a fun story of evolution) and the National Dairy Museum, which tells the story of the dairy industry since Waterloo.

On the floor of the entrance hall of Stratfield Saye House are two fine mosaics from the Roman town of **Silchester**. Its ruins lie 2 miles to the west, amidst open countryside. The entire site was sold to the county by the present Duke of Wellington in 1972. There may not at first sight be much to see (a stretch of Roman wall, the remains of an amphitheatre), but the site has been extensively excavated and the findings are well displayed in a small museum to the west. This is best reached from Basingstoke via the A340, turning right at Pamber End, then via Little London to Silchester. A path runs from the museum across the site and around the south-east section of the wall, in places 15ft high.

South-east of Silchester, on the other side of the Aldermaston Road, is **Pamber Priory**, an immensely peaceful spot reached by turning west at Pamber End, towards Charter Alley and Ramsdell. The church lies back from the road, beside a farm. The surviving building has been fashioned from the original presbytery and tower of the priory of Monk Sherborne, founded in 1101 by Henry of Port, who was seated at Basing. He granted the priory to a French abbey situated near his Norman homelands, at Cerisy-la-Forêt.

One of the great treasures to be found near Basingstoke is **the Vyne**, at Sherborne St John, a grand mansion owned by the National Trust. It is a feast for the connoisseur and anyone remotely interested in country houses. The original house was built in the early 16th century by William Sandys, courtier and soldier, whose descendants lived there until 1653. The Civil War dented the family fortunes and the house was sold to Chaloner Chute, a successful lawyer and Speaker of the House of Commons. His finely carved memorial (not tomb) is in a chamber off the chapel. Amongst the many changes he ordered was the addition of the fine Classical portico, the first in a country house anywhere in England. John Chute (1701–76), the last of the direct male line, was a designer friend of Horace Walpole of strawberry gothic fame, who used the 'Strawberry Parlour' when he stayed at the Vyne. This room leads off the Stone Gallery, which now serves as a visitors' hall. Its counterpart upstairs (reached via the stunning Classical staircase designed by John Chute) is the Oak Gallery, a long room that is fitted with Tudor linenfold panelling.

Another fine house within easy reach of Basingstoke is **Highclere Castle** (reached via the A339, turning left down the A34 and right after 2 miles). It is one of the largest houses in Hampshire. At first sight it looks like the Houses of Parliament, which is not surprising as they shared the same architect, Sir Charles Barry, who designed the mansion for the 3rd Earl of Carnarvon in about 1840. Its fabulously rich interiors in a variety of styles are by Thomas Allom and date from about 1860. The 5th Earl, who is buried on nearby Beacon Hill, financed Howard Carter's famous exploration of the Valley of the Kings in the 1920s. Finds from the tomb of Tutankhamun and other sites are displayed in a room in the house. The site of Highclere Castle was originally that of a palace of the bishops of Winchester. The grounds were laid out by Capability Brown in about 1775.

A surprising treasure well worth visiting at nearby Burghclere is the Sandham Memorial Chapel. Its walls were painted in the 1930s by

Highclere Castle

Jane Austen (1775–1817)
On the face of it, the literary achievements of Jane Austen are made all the more remarkable by the fact that for much of her time she led the life of the daughter of a country parson. However, the vitality that she brought to her work and the extent of her travels emphasise that life in the country in the last century was not necessarily one of isolation.

Jane was fortunate to come from a large family with a large circle of friends. They filled her life and gave her much of the material she later worked into her novels. Also, although she lived her early years in the remote village of Steventon, in north Hampshire, she attended schools in Southampton, Oxford and Reading. She went to balls and had a full social life in the country. She was also in touch with events in the world at large, especially through her brothers, two of whom were serving naval officers. Even the events of the French Revolution were brought home to her, when in 1794 the husband of one of her cousins was guillotined.

Most of her writing was completed at Chawton, where in 1809 at the age of 33 she went to live with her mother and sister Cassandra. *Sense and Sensibility*, *Mansfield Park*, *Pride and Prejudice* and *Emma*, which the Prince of Wales asked to be dedicated to him, were all completed during her time in this tiny village near Alton.

Stanley Spencer (1891–1959). They depict the humble realities of conflict, as recalled by the artist, who served as a hospital orderly in Macedonia during World War I.

This part of Hampshire is hill-walking territory. It is crossed by the Wayfarer's Walk, a long-distance footpath that threads round Beacon Hill beside the A34, over Ladle Hill opposite, and on to **Watership Down**, which was made famous by Richard Adams's bestselling story of rabbits. The book is based on real settings, like Sandleford, beside the River Enborne, which forms the county boundary hereabouts for several miles.

North-west of Basingstoke is the pretty village of **Wootton St Lawrence**, which has a surprising link with Jane Austen. Amongst the memorials in the local church is one to the local land-owner Harris Bigg-Wither, who in 1802 proposed to and was accepted by the young novelist. But she changed her mind overnight! She was living at Bath at the time, though her birthplace and for many years her family home was at Steventon, 4 miles to the south-west. The church her father served is still there, but the only trace of the rectory, which stood to the north, is an iron pump (a replacement of the original) in the middle of a field.

On the other side of the M3 from Steventon is a village that has been put on the map by a lady of another kind. This is 'Royal' **Dummer**, the home of 'Fergie', Sarah Ferguson, Duchess of York. The aptly named Queen Inn has become a good place to catch up on Palace chit-chat.

ALTON

'Sweet FA' is Alton's unflattering contribution to the English vernacular. It refers to Fanny Adams, a local girl gruesomely murdered in 1867. She lies in the cemetery in Old Odiham Road.

Most of Alton is contained in its long main

street. From the south, this runs beside the pleasant sward of the Butts and then through the main shopping centre and past a number of landmarks (all on the right): the Curtis Museum, the rail station (served by both BR and the steam locos of the Mid-Hants Railway), the hospital (beside the fine surviving workhouse of 1793) and the original Eggar's Grammar School, founded in 1641 by John Eggar of Crondall. The new school built in 1968 is further out of the town, at Holybourne. On the southern outskirts of the town is the Lord Mayor Treloar Hospital, orginally founded to care for the wounded in the Boer War, and the modern sports centre (three pools and a waterslide).

There are more shops in Market Street (with its attractive small Market Square), which leads west from the centre of the town and becomes Lenten Street. The River Wey rises in this quarter of the town, though you could easily come to Alton without realising it had a river.

The Alton story began at Neatham, now a tiny hamlet to the north-east. Here a significant Roman settlement called *Vindomis* grew up. Its importance is reflected in the fact that Alton was once in the Hundred of Neatham. The full story of Alton, from the Ice Age to the Restoration, is told in the Curtis Museum. The prime exhibit is the Alton Buckle, a fabulous piece of Saxon craftsmanship recovered from a local cemetery (AD525–625) in the south of the town. The museum also contains an interesting collection of toys, dolls and games, and a traditional display that includes relics of the town's brewing industry. Alton Pale Ale was once world famous. Local breweries have been swallowed up by Watneys and Courage, and Bass are now the only brewers in town. Some hops are still grown near Alton; but redundant oast-houses are a familiar sight. Paper Mill Lane is a relic of a former Alton industry.

Brewing and breweries
Until the coming of the railway, every town and many a village had its own brewery. Better communications meant that beer could be distributed from large breweries, where economies of scale could be realised. Thus, whereas at the turn of the century there were more than 80 separate breweries in Hampshire, today there are just two. One of these is the modern Bass plant at Alton and the other is the traditional brewery of Gale and Company at Horndean, which is still independent.

There is a third brewery in the county, at Southwick behind the Golden Lion pub. A celebratory brew was made here in 1985, when the brewery was restored, but it has now been put back 'under wraps'. It can be visited by special arrangement (telephone: 0705 380978). Southwick Brewhouse is a perfect example of what the small village brewery used to be like, when one man would make a few hundred gallons of ale with equipment that required a great deal of personal experience (and encouragement!) to operate.

In traditional brewing, malt is crushed and soaked in hot water in the 'mash tun' to make the 'wort'. This is then mixed with hops and sugar in a copper vessel and passed to the 'hop-back', where the hops are filtered off and the wort allowed to cool before passing finally to a fermentation vat.

industry. King's Pond was the mill pond and now forms a small area of nature conservation in the centre of the town.

The Curtis Museum takes its name from William Curtis (1746–99), the most famous member of a local family of apothecaries and doctors which came to the town in 1720. He worked in London, where he became a well-known botanist. Curtis's *Botanical Magazine*, founded in 1787, is still published. It is famous for its plates of flowers, which were coloured by hand until the 1950s.

Facing the museum is Church Street, which includes the Allen Gallery. This is strong on ceramics and silverware and has a delightful garden. It is famous for the Tichborne Spoons, a fine set of 'Apostle spoons', which date from 1592 but take their name from the regicide Sir Robert Tichborne (d.1682), a Hampshire man who was Lord Mayor of London during Cromwell's rule. Alton church, which faces down Church Street, was the scene of bloody fighting during the Civil War. The Royalist leader Colonel Richard Boles was hacked down in its pulpit. There is a memorial plate to him inside the church, on a pillar facing the south entrance.

Alton church is served by monks from the Anglican Benedictine community of Alton Abbey, which is at Beech, 2 miles to the south-west. It was founded in 1884 and set up on its present site a few years later, when a small group of monks from Barry, South Wales, came on foot to build a temporary church and abbey in wattle and daub. Originally founded to care for retired merchant seamen, the abbey now provides a home for elderly men from all walks of life. It also has a guest house.

The village of **Chawton**, just to the south of Alton, is famous as the home of Jane Austen (from 1806 to 1817). The house where she lived until almost the end of her life, and where some of her major works were written, still

stands. Administered by the Jane Austen
Memorial Trust, it was given by a father in
memory of his son, who was killed in action in
the last war. The house has been restored to
resemble its state in the early years of the last
century, when Jane and some of her family
came here after four unsettled years. They
came at the invitation of Jane's brother Edward,
who had had the fairy-tale experience of being
adopted by Mr and Mrs Thomas Knight, a
distantly related, wealthy but childless couple,
with estates in Kent and Hampshire.

After savouring the atmosphere of Jane's
cottage – her donkey cart and the table she
wrote at – it is well worth taking a short stroll
to view Chawton House, which is on the
eastern side of a quiet cul-de-sac to the south.

Oast houses, Isington

Edward, who took the name Knight,
eventually came to live here. The church and
graveyard beside the great house, where his
descendants still live, are full of Knight
memorials. Jane's mother and her sister
Cassandra are buried in the south-east part of
the churchyard. Jane herself is buried in
Winchester Cathedral

The Wey Valley between Alton and
Farnham is an area of pleasant meadows, old
manor houses and mills. **Froyle** has been called
'the village of saints', after the religious statues
set up on estate cottages by the last active lord
of the manor, Sir Hubert Miller, who died in
1941. The splendid manor house at Upper
Froyle is essentially Elizabethan with medieval
traces and later additions. It is now used by the
Lord Mayor Treloar College for handicapped
boys.

On the other side of the busy A31 is
Isington Mill, with its converted oast-houses,
where 'Monty', Viscount Montgomery of
Alamein, settled after the war. He died in 1976
and is buried nearby at Binsted.

Bentley on the A31 has an interesting
connection with the founder of the Boy Scout

Aldershot

Population: 32,654

Early Closing: Wed

Market Day: Thu

Cashpoints: *Barclays* 101
Victoria Rd; *Lloyds* 115
Victoria Rd; *Midland* 15
Wellington St; *NatWest* 117
Victoria Rd

Tourist Information:
Military Museum, Queen's
Avenue

Attractions: Airborne
Forces Museum, Royal
Corps of Transport
Museum

Arts: Prince's Hall, West
End Centre

Leisure: Aldershot
Stadium, Aldershot
Swimming Pools, Ice Rink,
Stainforth Ski Centre

Cinemas: Cannon Cinema

By Road: London 37 miles
(M3), Basingstoke 16 miles
(M3), Petersfield 20 miles
(A325)

By Rail: 50mins from
London (Waterloo to Alton
line)

movement, Lord Baden Powell (1857–1941).
Turn north at the crossroads in the centre of
the village, into Hole Lane (it is unsafe to stop
by the main road) and park behind the
memorial hall. Beside the A31 nearby is the
'Bentley Book', a potted history and sketch
map of the village under a small tile roof. It
was apparently designed in 1923 by Baden
Powell for a *Daily Mail* contest for the best
village sign. Half a mile up Hole Lane is Jenkyn
Place, which opens its gardens to the public.
On the north side of the house is a footpath
leading alongside Pax Hill, where the Chief
Scout lived.

The southern arm of the Bentley crossroads
leads to the visitors' centre of Alice Holt Forest
at Bucks Horn Oak (turn left at Blacknest).
Several miles of peaceful woodland walks, and
places to picnic. The southern part of the forest
is littered with the sites of Roman kilns. A
reconstructed kiln can be seen on the Goose
Green history trail. Authentic firings are
occasionally staged.

To the north-east, in a large clearing
surrounded by forest, is **Birdworld**, a hugh
bird zoo which is the creation of Roy Harvey.
In 1968 he gave up farming in Gloucestershire
to develop a consuming hobby. There are now
more than 40 separate enclosures containing a
vast variety of birds – parrots, vultures, storks,
flamingoes, macaws, cranes, penguins,
humming birds and many others. One
enclosure simulates the seashore, complete
with artificial beach, cliffs and waves.
Birdworld is fun for the family and paradise for
the bird buff. On the same site is Underwater
World, a sophisticated aquarium complex
stocked with a huge variety of fish from the
lakes, rivers and seas of the world. The tropical
sharks are so happy that they have bred, for
the first time in Britain.

ALDERSHOT AND FARNBOROUGH

The Borough of Rushmoor, which includes the towns of Aldershot and Farnborough, plus the military camp which separates them, was created in 1974. It took its name from Rushmoor Bottom. The military lands of Aldershot and district (including Bordon, Longmoor and Kingsley) are administered according to special bye-laws. These deny right of access to enclosed lands and allow the military authorities to order people off open lands (eg during exercises).

The wilderness that makes this part of the county ideal for field exercises and tank trials can also be found on the commons of Hawley, Yateley and other places further west. The valley of the River Blackwater, which stretches for 15 miles between Eversley and Farnham, has some good footpaths and plenty of old gravel workings for water-sports enthusiasts. The 55 acre Rowhill Nature Reserve is a pleasant area of woods, ponds and heathland around the source of the river.

Aldershot town (as distinct from the military town) is well provided with modern facilities. It has an ice rink, swimming pools, a dry-ski slope, an entertainments centre, a stadium (for greyhounds, stock-car, hot-rod and banger racing) and a good selection of modern shops (particularly in the Wellington Centre and Union Street). The ground of Aldershot Football Club is centrally placed at the east end of Victoria Road. To the south is the original village of Aldershot, including the park, manor house and parish church. The church tower dates from the 17th century and is built in brick and Bagshot 'brownstone'. Between the park and the church is the Heroes Garden, a war memorial decorated with stone from 52 places blitzed in the last war. There is some good architecture in Frederick Street (Culdrose House, 1860) and Queen's Street (Drysdale's Roman Catholic church of 1912–13).

Farnborough

Population: 48,294

Early Closing: Wed

Market Day: Tue

Cashpoints: *Lloyds* 66/68 Queensmead; *Barclays* 34/36 Victoria Rd; *Midland* 18 Alexandra Rd, 2 Victoria Rd; *NatWest* 2 Alexandra Rd

Tourist Information: The Library, Pinehurst

Arts: Prince Regent Theatre Club

Leisure: Farnborough Recreation Centre

By Road: London 34 miles (M3), Aldershot 2 miles

By Rail: 45mins from London (Waterloo to Basingstoke stopping service). Direct services from Farnborough to Basingstoke and Woking. Direct services from Farnborough North to Guildford and Reading.

Farnborough Abbey

Aldershot Military Camp
The first camp to be built at Aldershot, in 1853, was partly hutted and included barracks for cavalry. It straddled the Basingstoke Canal, whose fortunes were temporarily revived by the need to ferry vast quantities of building materials. The detailed story of the camp, up to the present day, is told in the Aldershot Military Museum, which is housed in two of the old barrack blocks.

Block M has displays that show events up to the start of the last war, together with a medal collection from 1815 to the present (with the exception of a medal from the Falklands Campaign). It also includes a reconstruction of a typical barrack room of about 1900. Block N chronicles the use of Aldershot by the Canadian Army, which took part in the disastrous Dieppe Raid of 1942.

In the 1930s Aldershot had lost it fighting divisions; it had become a huge training centre and was the home of the Parachute Regiment. After the war, thousands of men were posted to the camp during their National Service, a compulsory requirement until 1962.

Today, Aldershot camp has more than 90 units involved in training recruits and other functions. It is also the home of the 16th Parachute Brigade (called after the wartime 1st and 6th Brigades). In 1972 the brigade's officers' mess was bombed by Irish extremists and seven people were killed.

Aldershot is, of course, the home of the army. In 1853, just before the Crimean War, the land between Aldershot and Farnborough attracted the attention of military chiefs. They built a camp in this empty countryside, which was well-placed for both London and the south coast and had rail and canal links. Within six years Aldershot's civilian population had grown from less than 1,000 to 3,000, and it had acquired 60 taverns. By 1861, it had a population of nearly 17,000, of which 11,000 were army personnel.

The full story of Aldershot Camp is well told in the Aldershot Military Museum, which is in Queens Avenue inside the military town. Its modern displays are housed in the last of the two remaining single-storey brick late-Victorian barrack blocks. In the 1960s the camp began to be completely rebuilt in modern concrete 'boxes'.

There are seven other military museums in the Aldershot area, notably the Airborne Forces Museum in Alisons Road, which tells the story of the creation and operation of parachute forces from 1940 to the present. It has a large collection of aircraft models inside and a World War II Dakota outside. The other museums are rather specialised, and some have restricted opening hours. They cover (unless otherwise stated they are in Aldershot) transport, medicine (Ash Vale), physical training, dentistry, nursing, and ordnance (Camberley).

Aldershot has its share of quiet corners, like the woodland to the west of the A325 Farnborough Road. On a small knoll hereabouts is the Wellington Statue, a truly impressive bronze of the Waterloo hero on his horse Copenhagen. The 26ft monument was ousted from Hyde Park Corner and mounted at Aldershot in 1885. It overlooks the 120ft tower of the British Army Garrison Church.

Ideally **Farnborough** is best visited during its famous air show, which is staged in even years (1990, etc). The event is primarily a shop window for the Society of British Aerospace Companies. Safety is a prime concern and there has been no major accident involving the crowd since 1952, when 26 spectators were killed by a crashing de Havilland jet. The Royal Aircraft Establishment at Farnborough, founded in 1905 as 'His Majesty's Balloon Factory', is Europe's top centre for aerospace research. The best known of the early pioneers was 'Colonel' Sam Cody (1861–1913), the maverick Texan showman whose success with man-lifting kites led to his appointment as instructor to the Royal Engineers in 1904. In October 1908 he and an American Indian friend made the first sustained powered flight of an aircraft in the country in the aptly named British Aeroplane 1. They took off from Laffans Plain, near Farnborough, where Cody was killed in a crash five years later.

One landmark seen by pilots as they scream over Farnborough is St Michael's Abbey (actually a priory), an intriguing relic of the fall of the Second French Empire (1852–70) and its dictatorial emperor, Napoleon III, who fled to England. The abbey was built in 1887 by his widow, Empress Eugénie. She, her husband and their son, who was killed fighting for the British in the Zulu Wars, are buried here. The abbey was served by French Benedictines until the last war, when English monks from Prinknash took their place. The abbey, which has a craft shop, is entered from the east side of Farnborough Road, south of the station.

To the north is Farnborough Hill, built in about 1860 for the publisher T G Longman, and now used by a convent school. Empress Eugénie lived here from 1881 until her death in 1920.

Fleet is small town on the edge of Rushmoor but is in fact the administrative centre of the separate District of Hart, created in 1974. This is remarkable for a town which did not exist in 1840, when the first generation

Napoleon III and the Second French Empire
The Palmerston forts that ring Portsmouth Harbour were built to counter possible threats from the Second French Empire, under Napoleon III. It is ironic, therefore, that this man ended his days in England. At the end of the Franco-Prussian War (1870–1), he left France in defeat and came to live at Chislehurst in Kent. He died two years later and his widow went to live at Farnborough.

Two generations after the French Revolution, Napoleon III had struggled again and and again to establish his claim to imperial rule, until in 1848 he was elected to the French presidency. He subsequently dissolved the National Assembly and was elected president for ten years, with powers to rewrite the constitution. Soon he assumed the imperial crown and ruled France with dictatorial powers for almost 20 years.

At home, Napoleon III encouraged the building of railways and canals, improved trade and embellished Paris and other large towns. He also tried to improve the lot of the agricultural worker by providing better schooling.

Abroad, the new emperor followed an aggressive foreign policy, fighting in alliance with the English in the Crimea and China. In 1870 he underestimated the might of Prussia: the defeat of the French at Sedan spelt the end of his rule.

Charles Kingsley (1819–75)
Although the only well-known work of Charles Kingsley is *The Water Babies*, several other books of his are still in print. He was rector of Eversley, near Wokingham, from 1844 until his death in 1875. He still haunts the place: the graves of him and his wife are in the churchyard (south of the path), the Irish yews he planted still flank the path, the rectory in which he lived still stands. And there is a fine relief sculpture of him beneath the memorial on the east wall of the north aisle of the church, which was restored in his honour.

Born in the same year as Queen Victoria, he was a highly strung, very clever, slightly mixed-up man of the period. He annointed himself naked with briars, drew erotica, loathed Roman Catholicism and supported Christian Socialism (and would have done so even more vigorously if he had been able to tolerate the others who supported it!). For similar reasons, he withdrew his support from the Women's Rights Movement of John Stuart Mill, commenting shrewdly: 'I know, and have long foreseen, that what our new idea has to to beware of . . . is hysteria, male and female.'

For nine years Kingsley was Professor of Modern History at Cambridge, which was a royal appointment, yet he wrote such a vehemently anti-crown pamphlet at the time of the Crimean Way that it could not be published without risk of treason.

of commuters discovered the virtues of living in the country. Fleet is well served by shops and sports facilities but its main attraction is still its pond, the largest in the county. Apart from a small part at the west end, which was lopped off by the railway, it is still remarkably unspoilt. Woodland paths lead around the eastern part, which can be reached via Westover Road and Fugelmere Road (called after the Saxon, meaning 'wildfowl lake').

The northern parishes of Hart contain vast areas of delightful heathy countryside. **Hawley Common**, which is covered by the military bye-laws spreads around a large pond and is criss-crossed by footpaths. Yateley Country Park, which is owned by the county, covers 500 acres of common land and has three car parks, each beside a pond. The main one is in **Yateley** itself (at Wyndham's Pond off Cricket Hill Lane), where a lily-padded pond is set amidst heather commons and wood of silver birch. There are also car parks alongside the north-bound carriageway of the A30, at Stroud's Pond and beside a gravel pit.

Yateley village has a recently discovered Saxon church. Part of the structure was dated to the 11th century after repairs in 1952 revealed long-and-short work, but even more of the old church was found after a fire in 1979.

The church at nearby **Eversley** is also well worth a visit. The Victorian writer Charles Kingsley (1819–75) was rector of the parish for 31 years and is commemorated in the church. There is also a tablet to the architect John James (1672–1746), pupil of Sir Christopher Wren, whose own country mansion, Warbrook House, stands about a mile to the north-west. Eversley church and the rectory where Kingsley and his wife lived stand in an isolated position to the south of the main village. It is good walking country, once the haunt of squatters and deer poachers and now much sought after by commuters.

FURTHER READING

V.G. Beddington and E.B. Christy,
It Happened in Hampshire,
Hampshire Federation of
Women's Institutes, 1977 (fifth
edition)

**P. Brough, R. Gibbons and C.
Pope,**
*The Nature of Hampshire and the Isle
of Wight,*
1986, Barracuda Books

B. Carpenter Turner,
A History of Hampshire,
Phillimore, 1978 (second edition)

W. Cobbett,
Rural Rides,
1830, Penguin edition, 1967

J. Duthy,
Sketches of Hampshire,
Laurence Oxley, 1839, reprinted
1973

R. Dutton,
Hampshire,
Batsford, 1970

G. Hedley and A. Rance,
*Pleasure Grounds: The Gardens and
Landscapes of Hampshire,*
Milestone Publications, 1987

J. Holder and B. Shurlock,
Explore Hampshire,
Hampshire County Council, 1986
(third edition)

W.H. Hudson,
Hampshire Days,
1903, reprinted Barry Shurlock,
1973

M. Hughes,
The Small Towns of Hampshire,
Hampshire Archaeological
Committee, 1976

A. Mee (editor),
Hampshire with the Isle of Wight
(The King's England),
Hodder and Stoughton, 1939

J. Munby (editor),
Hampshire (Domesday Book)
Phillimore, 1982

N. Pevsner and D. Lloyd,
*The Buildings of England:
Hampshire and the Isle of Wight,*
Penguin, 1967

R. Potter,
Hampshire Harvest,
Phillimore, 1977

**S.J. Shennan and R. T. Schadla
Hall (editors),**
Archaeology of Hampshire,
Hampshire Field Club, 1981

T.W. Shore,
History of Hampshire,
Elliot Stock, 1892

B. Shurlock,
Portrait of the Solent,
Robert Hale, 1983

C.R. Tubbs,
The New Forest,
New Naturalist Series, Collins,
1986

R.V. Turley (editor), *Hampshire
and Isle of Wight Bibliographies,*
Barry Shurlock, 1975

G. White,
The Natural History of Selborne,
Benjamin White, 1789

Some of the above may be out of
print but should be still available
from libraries.